How to Implement
Information Systems
and Live to Tell About It

How to Implement Information Systems and Live to Tell About It

Howard Fallon

A Wiley–QED Publication

John Wiley & Sons, Inc.

New York • Chichester • Brisbane • Toronto • Singapore

Publisher: Katherine Schowalter
Editor: Theresa L. Hudson
Managing Editor: Mark Hayden
Composition: Publishers' Design and Production Services, Inc.

This text is printed on acid-free paper.

This publication is designed to provide accurate and authoritative information in regard to the subject matter covered. It is sold with the understanding that the publisher is not engaged in rendering legal, accounting, or other professional services. If legal advice or other expert assistance is required, the services of a competent professional person should be sought. FROM A DECLARATION OF PRINCIPLES JOINTLY ADOPTED BY A COMMITTEE OF THE AMERICAN BAR ASSOCIATION AND A COMMITTEE OF PUBLISHERS.

Library of Congress Cataloging-in-Publication Data:

Fallon, Howard, 1948–
    How to implement information systems and live to tell about it /
Howard Fallon.
        p.   cm.
    Includes index.
    ISBN 0-471-01876-7 (paper)
    1. System design.   2. Electronic data processing.   3. Management
information systems.   I. Title.
QA76.9.S88F35   1994
004'.068'4—dc20   94-13974
                                                                              CIP

Printed in the United States of America
10 9 8 7 6 5 4 3 2 1

Contents

Acknowledgments

The implementation of any product or system is a collaborative and cooperative effort. I would like to acknowledge those people without whom this project would never have been implemented into the hardcopy you hold in your hands today. I am grateful to Terri Hudson, my editor at John Wiley. While Terri's title is "editor," in actuality she *coordinated* all aspects of the process so that my proposal could be *implemented* into this book. Terri's efforts are a great statement about the value and importance of a project having an Implementation Coordinator (IC). I thank the following information systems professionals who gave graciously of their time and provided me with valuable insights and much of the anecdotal material: Rosemary Criste-Baldwin, Marilynn Hall, Donna Rund, Patricia Seymour, Hassan Sharif, and Julie Wilson. My thanks go to Anna Gadsby for drawing the chapter cover illustrations and to Kim Dahl of Micrografx for giving me Micrografx Designer, which I used to produce the graphics. A special thanks to Ed Buryn for editing, direction, and support.

Preface

This book is directed at anyone responsible for, or interested in, the detailed process of implementing information systems. While there are a plethora of books covering all phases of the System Development Life Cycle (SDLC) and numerous books on particular aspects of this cycle—such as planning, analysis, design, programming, testing, and quality—this is the first book to address the *specifics of implementation*.

This book describes with examples and anecdotes the role of the Implementation Coordinator (IC) and the Joint Implementation Process (JIP). If you learn the role and responsibilities of the IC, and utilize the JIP process as presented in this book, you will be able to deal with the complexities of coordinating numerous people and technologies in the pursuit of a successful implementation.

Figure P.1 is a symbolic representation of the communication and coordination that must be exercised for an implementation to be successful. This book will show you how to facilitate communication and coordinate all aspects of the implementation effort.

INDUSTRY TRENDS

With the trend in business toward downsizing and restructuring, managers are scrambling to justify their value to the organization. Just having a span of control over a certain number of people isn't enough anymore. With the demise of the hierarchical organizational structure, companies no longer want managers to keep an eye on subordinates, fill out their yearly reviews, and direct their professional development. In the newly decentralized and self-di-

Figure P.1.   **Communication/Coordination Wheel**

rected organizations of today, companies expect management personnel to prove that they are adding value to the business. What companies are looking for are the "soft skills" of orchestration, coordination, and facilitation. By learning and practicing these skills as presented in this book, you can substantiate your usefulness to the organization.

EMPLOYEE VS. CONSULTANT

Although I work as a consultant on a contract basis, I know you don't have to be an outsider to be an effective Implementation Coordinator. In fact, most of the professionals I interviewed for anecdotal material were employees of their organizations. Therefore, the information contained herein is valid for anyone who wants to coordinate an implementation. Whether you're an employee or a consultant, the essential requirements are the same: a desire to work with people, the perseverance to solve problems, and a love of new challenges.

IMPLEMENTATION COORDINATOR SUPPORT

Being an Implementation Coordinator can be one of the most arduous and thankless jobs in the world. So, as a gesture of professional commiseration, I encourage you to contact me by electronic mail if you crave some support or seek critical feedback. I can be reached at:

COMPUSERVE at Howard Fallon, 76267,457
INTERNET at 76267.457@compuserve.com

AUTHOR'S NOTE

While many of the "stories" in this book are drawn from the author's experience, an equal number are based on interviews with professional colleagues in the information systems industry. My intent is to give the book a broad-based perspective.

A troublesome grammatical issue I encountered while writing this book was choosing between "he" and "she" for indefinite pronouns. And yet to say "they" instead would have been incorrect. For consistency of prose and product I finally chose to use the feminine gender for all indefinite pronouns in this book. Using the feminine gender for all the anecdotal material also supports the anonymity of those professionals I interviewed.

ABOUT THE AUTHOR

Howard Fallon has worked in the information systems industry for more than 25 years as a Programmer, Systems Designer, Project Manager, and Implementation Coordinator for many *Fortune 1000* corporations. Since 1986 he has been president of his own consulting firm, the Kilton Peele Company, Inc., which published his first book, *Managing Projects Instead of People: A Strategy for Getting Results*. From his book, the author developed a seminar entitled "Recasting the Role of Project Management" that he has presented to corporations and governmental agencies across the country. The author frequently speaks to professional organizations such as the Association of Computing Machinery (ACM), Association of Systems Management (ASM), Data Processing Management Association (DPMA), and Independent Computer Consulting Association (ICCA). He lives in San Francisco, California, with his wife Julee, an Information Systems Analyst, and their two young daughters, Shane and Kendra.

CHAPTER 1

Introduction

In plain talk and without sugar, this book describes in detail the job of the Implementation Coordinator within the information systems industry, and tells you exactly how to implement a complex information system or product even though it crosses many organizational boundaries and hardware platforms.

In today's distributed, multi-platform environment, every computer from palmtops to mainframes will be sharing information and resources. The tried and tested project-management techniques that work well for the design, coding, testing, and installation of a stand-alone information system are not sufficient for an implementation in distributed and cooperative processing environments. This book presents the simple but numerous truths about the complex task of orchestrating the successful implementation of an information system into today's hardware-heterogeneous, cross-organizational corporate environments.

System implementation is "where the rubber meets the road." Although many books and seminars on project management espouse the principles and practices of successful project management, most of the tools and techniques they present focus on the front-end of the project life-cycle. This is obvious concerning planning, design, and specification, but even testing and quality assurance are activities that address *what* the system will do, not *how* it will be implemented. This book, however, addresses the implementation issues on the back-end of the life cycle. Typically, the end of a project finds the initial enthusiasm flagging, disillusionment creeping in, and the non-contributors looking for a way to get off the project, especially now that the really tough issues must be faced.

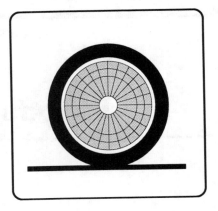

One of the most common occurrences in this industry is to have a great idea or plan fail in its implementation. The theory was valid but its implementation impossible—screwed up due to mistakes, mismanagement, misunderstandings, and mysterious gremlins. Yet this need not be so. In fact, the challenge is what makes implementation FUN. It's where things get done! You get no kicks or kudos from idling around with thoughts, plans, hopes, and dreams. What's really gripping, and what makes all the difference, is *what gets implemented.*

> *One of the shortcomings of American corporations is [that] they focus far too much on strategy and not nearly enough on* <u>*implementation.*</u>
>
> —David Kearns

WHAT YOU WILL LEARN

This book describes the roles and responsibilities of the Implementation Coordinator (IC), the person who coordinates all aspects of the implementation and facilitates the Joint Implementation Process (JIP) Sessions. JIP Sessions are a specific type of workshop for handling meetings that are pertinent to the implementation. Because meetings are among the most complex activities happening within any organization, JIP Sessions provide an explicit process and forum for producing success. This book presents in detail the practical applications of many different types of JIP Sessions.

THE KEYS TO SUCCESS

If you can control the implementation effort, your chances for success will increase. Therefore, gaining control is of utmost importance. In my parlance, a *key* is a technique that serves as a means of *control*.

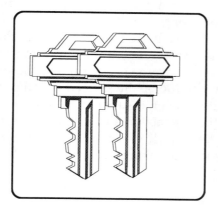

The First Key

The first key to implementation success is to build the new or revised system's *credibility* in such a way that you gain the necessary political support. Building support for a large implementation is especially difficult because it typically crosses many divisional and organizational boundaries within—and sometimes even outside— the corporation. Most of the major implementation issues involve the *culture* of the organization, so building support is essential to the implementation's success.

> About 95 percent of information-technology application issues involve power and organization, <u>not technology</u>. Since these issues are largely political, start to work through them <u>now</u> because they're on the "critical path" for <u>implementation</u>.
>
> —Tom Peters

The IC builds support by approaching the power and organizational issues through JIP Sessions that address concerns and build consensus. JIP Sessions are described in Chapter 4.

The Second Key

The second key to success is shrinking the time needed to accomplish the implementation. Organizations want to implement new systems or reengineer existing systems in a timely manner. In today's marketing environment a company's product mix cannot remain effective over a long period of time. To stay competitive, organizations must not only be sensitive to the market, but deliver systems with a sense of urgency, understanding that competing within an acceptable time frame is essential to the success of every organization. Otherwise the business need that the system seeks to address may truncate or even disappear entirely.

ICs emphasize the urgency of addressing the technological and organizational hurdles via JIP Sessions that identify issues, define objectives, and resolve problems promptly. JIP Sessions are described in Chapter 4.

IMPLEMENTATION PROBLEMS

ICs find that most implementation problems deal with communication and coordination. These areas are fraught with ambiguities that create mismatched or misunderstood expectations. It's difficult to get things right even when all parties to an agreement believe they've achieved mutual understanding. Technological problems stand in contrast to communication and coordination problems. Technological problems, whether they involve hardware and/or software, reside in environments with predefined rules, so it is a straightforward process to research the situation and determine the best possible alternatives. There is little equivocation. When they are dreaming, ICs wish every implementation would have only technological problems, because they know that in real life it's the communication and coordination problems that get you in the end.

There are no technological problems.

—IC truism

THE END GAME

It's probably true that there are few people in the information systems industry who haven't been exposed to some form of project-management training. However, this training typically addresses only those aspects unique to the inception of the project, such as planning, estimating, staffing, scheduling, and so forth.

With this in mind, let's look at the game of chess. Many people have a rudimentary knowledge of the rules and the movement of the pieces on the chess board. They typically know at least one opening move and can "play the game." But can they checkmate their opponent? The difference between swapping pieces on the board and checkmating your opponent is like night and day. The game gets harder as fewer pieces remain on the board because that situation creates many more possibilities. Few players have had the opportunity to develop a good "end game."

The analogy between the chess game and project management is apropos. Everyone understands, through both experience and training, how to get a project going. But how much literature and training is available about how to get a system or product implemented into the production environment at crunch time? The fact of the matter is that, as a professional IC, you need to develop a good "end game" for your project, because it can make all the difference in whether you will be able to get your system or product implemented.

JIPS AND ICS: A GOOD COMBO

The complex world of information systems unfortunately deals with software that often represents vague business principles. Therefore, we need a process for combining technology and business that is consistent, repeatable, and effective. Joint Implementation Process (JIP) Sessions are such a process. It's the theme of this book that you can "JIP" your way to implementation success by understanding how to effectively use JIP Sessions. Figure 1.1 is a symbolic representation of the three things an IC must do for a JIP Session to be successful.

ICs love facilitating JIP Sessions because:

1. They're "doers" who really want to see something achieved.
2. They have a knack for coordinating energies "on the fly."
3. They like being in front of a crowd.

Figure 1.1.   JIP Session Wheel

THE POWER OF THE INDIVIDUAL

People influence the world. People get things done. And people get systems and products implemented. Methodologies, processes, and procedures will not get a system or product implemented. While JIP is an important process, without the IC the process is useless. A competent IC utilizing the JIP process is a force to be reckoned with. An incompetent IC who uses JIP or any other process will be ineffectual and maybe even dangerous.

THE BASIC PRECEPTS

The material presented in this book isn't chiseled in stone. ICs are learning and adapting every day. If you understand the role of the IC and the theory behind JIP, you should be able to adapt these techniques to your own implementation. Figure 1.2 is a symbolic representation of the basic precepts an IC would do well to always remember:

Figure 1.2.   **Coordination/Communication Wheel**

CHAPTER 2

What's an Implementation Coordinator?: The Business Case for an IC

The Implementation Coordinator (IC) is the person who makes sure the product or system is implemented in the operational environment in a timely manner. In today's rapidly changing business climate, organizations simply cannot survive if they don't implement systems on time. The IC is the person who drives a stake in the ground and attaches everyone to it; centering the project makes everyone accountable to the due date. Without this focus, an implementation could easily drift past its delivery date, to the detriment of the entire organization and despite everyone's positive intentions and efforts.

WHY IS THE IMPLEMENTATION COORDINATOR NEEDED?

The concept of the Implementation Coordinator is still relatively unknown, so this is a question that senior management often asks. Typically the Project Manager responds, "Because she keeps us from going around in circles." This roundabout answer means that the IC is the person who usually brings the Project Manager's attention to impasses that require the Project Manager's attention or decisions. A more rational answer is that the IC is a professional "go-between" who manages the logistics of intercommunicating highly technical data among the information systems personnel who accomplish the implementation. Think of an implementation as a high-tech talent show with the IC acting as the MC or Master of Ceremonies, with Matrix Consciousness.

WHO'S LOOKING OUT FOR YOUR INTERESTS?

By their very nature, organizations tend to become *compartmentalized*, and groups within them tend to assume that other groups will always take care of them. Yet this is seldom the case. For instance, are the required resources for which other groups are responsible going to be available in time for your implementation? Think about things like disk space, processing cycles, operational support for after-business hours or weekends, and the like. By contrast, ICs deliberately assume no one is looking out for their implementation's interests. They know that they have to get out and beat the bushes to make sure that whatever resources their implementation requires are going to be available when the time comes.

HOW OFTEN DO ORGANIZATIONS ACTUALLY UTILIZE AN IC?

Virtually every project has someone coordinating the implementation, yet few organizations formalize the role with the title of "Implementation Coordinator." Some of the titles that are used are: Product Implementation Manager or Project Implementation Manager. However, you'll usually find that practicing ICs bear titles that seem inappropriate—such as Senior Systems Engineer, Quality Assurance Officer, or Business Systems Analyst. Since people are usually known more for their functional contribution than their formal title, a person's title may not signify their true role on a project. (This is why organizational charts are often misleading.) Therefore, although the title may not fit, the role of IC is much in evidence.

WHEN DOES THE IMPLEMENTATION COORDINATOR START?

Typically, there is nothing typical about when the IC starts the job. The IC can be of use at any point in the project from the initial Feasibility Study to the point at which the Project Manager has crashed the implementation. So there isn't any particular point in the System Development Life Cycle at which to say, "Now for the IC!" However, the sooner the IC is brought into any project, the better it will be for all concerned. Even at the Feasibility Study stage, major implementation issues need to be addressed. Once the IC is on site, issues of concern can immediately begin to be identified, assigned, and dealt with in an efficient manner.

> *Rule of Thumb: The sooner the IC is brought in, the better.*

ABOUT SYSTEMS SHOPS

The need for ICs is usually evident in decentralized organizations. Decentralized organizations typically have autonomous units with information systems that must act in concert with other units' information systems to achieve the information processing necessary for the organization's goals. So by their very nature decentralized organizations have inherent difficulties in coordinating an implementation to accomplish their objectives. However, ICs are also valuable in traditional hierarchical organizations. These large, monolithic systems shops often have "dead zones" within the responsibility matrix. Moreover, many of their managers and programmers work harder for the survival of the systems shop than the success of the business user. Because the IC is more constrained in these organizations, her challenge is to instigate and creatively build the political support necessary to champion the particularized work that will ensure a successful implementation.

SYSTEMS BACKGROUND

The information systems industry is a vast technological cornucopia of complex concepts and hardware with terminology to match. Therefore it goes without saying that the IC must be trained and experienced, a computernik who speaks computerese with a pronounced systems accent. Beyond that, the IC must be able to ask cogent and sometimes uncomfortable questions, know who to ask them of, and be able to constructively decode the answers. An effective IC needs both knowledge and enough gumption to be able to tell the Project Manager, "By golly gee, I think you're heading in the wrong direction." Technical competence is required because the IC often directs the implementation, in effect becoming the channel

pilot who uses her knowledge to steer the ship of implementation between the sandbars that lie hidden within the tasking maze.

ORGANIZATIONAL STRUCTURES

Most implementation efforts are accomplished in temporary horizontal work groups that function like task forces. These work groups or teams preempt the organization's hierarchy and cut across the traditional lines of command by bringing together as *peers* those persons necessary to accomplish a given task. These autonomous teams, known for their expediency and flexibility, are protean—capable of forming, disbanding, and reforming all through the implementation. These teams also interact with other implementation teams to form networks that continually expand and contract to fulfill implementation requirements and to resolve problems situationally. Without an IC to orchestrate and coordinate this transitory organizational structure of horizontal teams and expanding and contracting networks, the implementation effort risks a gradual degeneration into total chaos.

SELF-DIRECTED WORK TEAMS

Because they are effective in increasing creativity and productivity, the Self-Directed Work Team organizational structure is becoming popular in the modern corporate environment. A Self-Directed

Work Team is a group of professionals who are equally responsible for completing a task or delivering a product. Since each member of the team has greater autonomy and decision-making authority, the need for the traditional "line manager" to make each and every decision is eliminated. In this organizational structure the manager's job is being eliminated. However, just because the team doesn't need someone to make their decisions, that doesn't mean they don't need someone to "work the issues." Self-Directed Work Teams will fail unless they have ICs to accept responsibility for the issues and make sure that those issues get resolved.

When ICs work on implementations employing Self-Directed Work Teams they invariably find the members of the teams saying, "Thank goodness you're here! We need these issues resolved." Team members are usually technical specialists (such as programmers, analysts, database administrators, and so forth) who have their own specialized work to do, and lack time and incentive to run around the organization resolving each issue. The team members need to get closure on all the open issues being raised by their efforts, and know the value of an Implementation Coordinator who can focus on doing just that.

Once upon an implementation, Group A was modifying an Artificial Intelligence (AI) system that was designed to interface cross-county with another AI system being modified by Group B. Since the organization had Self-Directed Work Teams there were no managers. Six months into the project, Group B lost its single source of integrated responsibility. One day, someone heretofore unknown called Group A and said, "Hi, my name is Brand Noo and I've taken over the responsibilities of Bea Gonne. She left this note on her desk with your phone number on it, so I thought I'd call and see what you folks are doing!" Needless to say, Group A was beside itself. A bona-fide Implementation Coordinator was soon brought in, and her first directive from Group A was to find out what was happening with Group B. Group B needed to define its responsibilities and assert its contributions to the implementation. If necessary, the IC was prepared to escalate the issue to senior management to make sure that someone in Group B "cared enough to give the very best" to the implementation of the interface between the two AI systems.

MEETINGS

Meetings are the work arenas of any implementation. Through *conversation with our peers*, the inconsistencies in our assumptions are disclosed and innovative solutions are generated. Joint Implementation Process (JIP) is a process used effectively by ICs to promote the *joint skills* of inquiry, learning, planning, and problem solving. It is essential to the success of every implementation that peers work in concert with one another.

> *JIP Sessions are a series of meetings facilitated by the IC over the course of the implementation to jointly determine the best possible course of action at every point.*
>
> *—IC's definition*

A feature of every implementation is that the environment is fluid. The situation changes daily and you need a forum to address the many unforeseen and multifarious problems as they are encountered. JIP Sessions work well with implementations because they provide the forum for problem solving and resolution. Figure 2.1 represents how in JIP Sessions the participants can decide *cooperatively*, and in a timely manner, just what needs to be done. This provides a foundation for realistic and updateable timelines, and resolves mismatched expectations.

> *The business we're in is more sociological than technological, more dependent on knowledge-worker's ability to communicate with each other than their abilities to communicate with machines.*
>
> *—Tom DeMarco & Tim Lister*

WHICH MEETINGS GET JIPPED?

Once an IC is working on an implementation, all meetings regarding the implementation are usually conducted as JIP Sessions under the auspices of the IC. The only difference between one JIP Session and another is the amount of pre-session planning and preparation, the number of attendees, and the tools used within the JIP Sessions.

Figure 2.1.   Joint Implementation Process

CREEPING IMPLEMENTATION SCOPE

"Creeping scope" or the gradual, unplanned increase in what exactly is to be implemented has been the bane of many an implementation. For example, you start out to implement a client/server application on a network and end up dealing with issues of database management for the entire enterprise. Creeping scope is not necessarily due to the arbitrary whims of the business user. It often simply reflects the fact that problems of the business world change faster than the implementors can devise solutions. Failure to control these changes seems endemic to the information systems industry, and if uncontrolled, they will wreak havoc on your implementation. JIP is a process that enables the IC to handle creeping scope: for everyone involved in the implementation, it creates consensus about what will and will not be done.

ICs find pricing and priorities to be effective controls upon unreasonable requests for increasing scope. By sitting the implementors down with the business users in a JIP Session, and jointly having the implementors quote prices while the business users enumerate priorities, the IC can coordinate a strategy for coping with the implementation's scope. Everyone in the JIP Session will understand what the deliverables are, when those deliverables are due, and the reasons and purposes behind the implementation strategy.

THE AGE OF SPECIALIZATION

In the olden days of yore, the Project Manager for a system's design, development, and implementation was typically someone from the MIS division. Since then, two fundamental changes have occurred in that paradigm.

First, the Project Manager is now someone from the business or user side of the organization. This is appropriate because the business people are the ones who fund and ultimately take responsibility for the system or product to be implemented, so they should be in charge.

Second, the role of the Project Manager has been subdivided into a number of specialized roles. Look at any sizable project today and you will see a number of different people performing duties that used to be solely the responsibility of the Project Manager. On the front-end of a project you have one or more Joint Application Development (JAD) facilitators and team builders. Over the life of the project, various other people are responsible for quality assurance and Total Quality Management (TQM). On the back-end of the project, yet other people are responsible for implementation coordination and training. These roles and their relationship to the Project Manager are represented in Figure 2.2. This figure presents just a few of the specialists now performing duties that were once solely the domain of the Project Manager.

Specialization is the natural response to complexity. The reason for the segmentation of the Project Manager's responsibilities is increasing complexity of the overall task. As the construction and implementation of information systems evolves and expands, so does the level of complexity. This in turn necessitates the segmentation and further specialization of the Project Manager's duties. Breaking a job down into discrete roles concentrates expertise on particular functions and promotes control by having individuals be accountable for individual functions.

THE IC IN RELATION TO THE PROJECT MANAGER

ICs don't characterize themselves as Project Managers because that implies ownership of the system. The IC is a proponent of the

JAD Facilitator   **Team Builder**

P R O J E C T   M A N A G E R

Quality Assurance   **Implementation Coordinator**

Figure 2.2.   **Project Manager Support Personnel**

system's implementation, not it's proprietor. In the organizational structure of today, the Project Manager is most often the business user who is accountable for the system. The proper relationship of the IC to the Project Manager is as the *chief ally*. The Project Manager provides leadership while the IC provides mentoring. The IC works hand-in-hand with the Project Manager, providing counsel and serving as a sounding board for ideas and opinions. In this management configuration, the IC disseminates information and coordinates energy.

THE PROJECT MANAGER'S RESPONSIBILITIES

Project Managers lack the luxury of working on only one objective at a time. Their forte is the art of multi-tasking: they do such things as staffing, making performance reviews, running charitable campaigns, holding staff meetings of every description, and much more. It's important for the organization—for both its structure and its history—that these things get done. By contrast, the IC isn't burdened with these responsibilities and can focus on the implementation itself.

> Once upon an implementation, the IC was brought onto a site at which the PM was responsible for an implementation that touched every application in the organization. The Project Manager was completely stressed out because she was trying to manage not just the project, but all the implementation issues and their incident effects. The IC liberated the Project Manager by taking on all the responsibilities of the implementation itself, while moving around the organization and establishing working relationships with every interfacing group. Not only did the IC salvage the Project Manager's sanity, she was able to ensure that the implementation received the coordination necessary to deliver the system on time.

THE PROJECT MANAGER AS USER

It's hard for a business user to be the Project Manager—which requires a certain level of detachment—and at the same time represent her own interests as the user of the system to be implemented. How do you fight for what you want and still be conciliatory toward those you want to do things for you? One way that works well is by having someone else intercede with those whose contributions you need. With an IC on the project the business user can aggressively campaign for what she wants, yet not be caught up in all the implementation issues. The business user doesn't have to be concerned about everyone working together toward the system's implementation. That's the IC's responsibility.

THE PROJECT MANAGER AS FACILITATOR

The Project Manager cannot lead a fair and non-manipulative JIP Session because she has a personal investment in the session's content and outcome. It's hard for the Project Manager to play the role of the person who makes the decisions *and* also plays the IC's role of making sure all the possibilities are voiced. These are opposite points of view, and no one should be expected to play both roles effectively. ICs know from experience that Project Managers who conduct their own JIP Sessions are the most active participants, which restricts energy, information, and consensus.

> *Managers typically talk on average more than 60 percent of the time in the meetings they lead.*
>
> —Michael Doyle & David Straus

THE IC AS FACILITATOR

The IC initiates, coordinates, and facilitates the JIP Sessions. Facilitating a JIP Session is more than conducting the proceedings in a nice, polite way. ICs are willing and knowledgeable enough to say, "Here is what we need." Therefore, professional ICs have a strong information systems background. The information systems industry can be abstruse and even obscure in its use of terminology and concepts. Its personnel will respect only someone who can command everyone's attention by being able to ask pertinent questions couched in professional knowledge. The IC must speak the language of computers and information systems, and be able to lead and follow conversations within a contextual frame of reference. A facilitator from Human Resources with no systems background would not do well leading a JIP Session.

THE IC'S AUTHORITY

ICs typically have no explicit authority whatsoever! Explicit authority devolves from the Project Manager and the organization's upper management. ICs have the *responsibility* for the implementation but no direct *authority* to make it happen. Responsibility without authority is the classic curse of control freaks, but is a constant, creative challenge to an IC. The IC's ace is JIP, which provides the forum in which to "push and pull." The IC jumps right in and helps some people, while making demands of others. For example, some

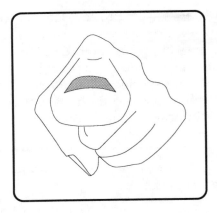

people in every organization can't be counted on to do their piece of the implementation within the needed timeframes. There are others who may never get their part done at all. So the IC is there to point the way, help out, or even kick butt. Sometimes the IC needs to escalate issues to the Project Manager and/or senior management, and at others they utilize friendly persuasion. Using their own judgment, ICs do whatever it takes to get the job done. Sometimes this gets them into trouble, but it's all part of being an IC and getting the system or product implemented.

IMPLEMENTATION COORDINATOR

Roles + Responsibilities

CHAPTER 3

The Implementation Coordinator: Roles and Responsibilities

In addition to being a technical specialist, the Implementation Coordinator organizes, coordinates, and facilitates the complex details of installing information systems into the operational business environment. An effective IC works fast, likes people, and works well with everyone—especially the Project Manager, whom the IC serves as informal implementation mentor. The IC must be quick-witted and yet even-tempered. The IC never (well, almost never) gets over-emotional, over-intellectual, or over-bureaucratic.

The IC enjoys lots of responsibility without much authority—so her success depends on being able to effectively *orchestrate* the implementation. The IC must know where the system "hurts" and what points, people, and problem areas need to be "massaged." She must persuade the right people to attend JIP Sessions and then be technically competent to understand what they say there. Systems personnel tend to be strong-willed and bright—so if the IC can't handle these types, she'll be in deep trouble.

As the person disseminating information and coordinating energy, the IC reviews all the documentation for the implementation and makes sure that everything is accounted for and correct. To do this, the IC must get the key participants to step forward and announce the requirements for their issues, and upon resolution, sign-off on those issues. The IC works the implementation issues and is responsible for the Issues Log. The Issues Log is described in Chapter 4.

ORCHESTRATION

Over the course of the implementation, and especially during a JIP Session, the IC must make many subliminal "judgment calls." These decisions can be characterized as *orchestration*, which is the skill of involving everyone, while maintaining the flow of information. In yet another performance metaphor, the IC is like an orchestra conductor, directing certain persons or sections to "come on stronger," while directing others to abate. Over the course of the "concert" these directions change for every individual and group many times.

One way to painlessly practice the techniques of orchestration is to host parties at which you actively promote the interactions of the guests and make sure everyone is relating well. When people who don't care for one another (usually relatives) wind up in the same corner, you tactfully separate them. If several people are engaged in meaningful dialogue that may be disrupted by an insensitive newcomer to the conversation, you diplomatically distract the interfering party. These situations and scenarios occur frequently at parties, so have a ball and at the same time practice and perfect your orchestration techniques. It's much tougher to learn on the job because your credibility is at stake. Also, if you ruffle feathers at your home party, no one is likely to complain because it's your turf—and besides, you paid for the amenities.

To be a good IC you must enjoy making things happen within a group. Loners need not apply. If you don't enjoy promoting amicability, then being an IC probably isn't for you. Remember that, from one point of view, being an IC is like being an MC—a rotten, thankless job. You do all the dirty work (arrangements, orchestration, clean-up) while everyone else—you hope—enjoys the function. So think about the implications of orchestration.

In any social context everyone has an idea—at least subliminally—about how much talking they should do. Different people expect to speak most of the time, some of the time, or hardly at all. Thus, one critical aspect of orchestration is allotting what people feel is their share of the conversation; otherwise they will feel slighted. The opposite is also true—if you force someone to speak much longer than they wish, that person will be angry at you because they have been overextended.

If someone starts using a JIP Session as a forum for venting some personal issue, it's up to you to get that person and/or issue offline. A typical example is the disgruntled employee who uses a meeting to express private complaints. Nothing could be more divisive or debilitating for a JIP Session. Be sympathetic, but don't let people go on about their particular gripes. When people go off on some tangent, it's usually because they're "over their head" as far as their particular responsibility is concerned, and they're really crying for help. To orchestrate effectively you must try to see inside situations and determine what's really the issue. Trust yourself to do the right thing, with the expectation that someone will tell you if you're wrong. Always remember that working with people is an inexact science at best.

Diversity Is Good

The IC must be sensitive to people's differences, and realize that everyone's convictions are right for them. The collaborative nature of JIP Sessions makes them excellent forums for expediting work in the modern organization. Through collaboration, people forge new understandings and discover that diversity brings fresh perspectives. JIP Sessions help everyone transcend their preconceived notions about what will (and will not) work.

Empowerment to the People

If they can have input into the implementation process, the participants gain a necessary sense of control. For example, in a manufacturing environment dedicated to quality, anyone can stop production. The workers on the line understand that their input affects the product. ICs try to instill that same consciousness in the implementation process. If the IC acts on feedback, the participants realize they have power within the implementation process. This is how an IC can transform *compliance* to *commitment*. Even in organizations without empowerment, ICs have still successfully empowered the participants within their implementations. Professionals are usually ready and willing to embrace good ideas.

Making a Presentation

When making a presentation, keep it as brief as possible. Typically, if you talk for over half an hour without interruption, you start losing people's interest. So it's best if you get your audience involved by asking questions, seeking clarification, and maybe even redirecting what you are presenting. You should be able to handle questions "on the fly" as long as they aren't too long or abusive. If a question is too long, tell the querist that you can speak with her personally after the presentation. If someone is negative or abusive toward you, let the audience handle your defense. The audience will invariably stand up for the speaker, and it really looks bad if the speaker goes after the antagonist.

How to Prepare a Presentation

The Audience:	Know to whom you are speaking.
The Bottom Line:	State your conclusions.
The Method:	Present your analysis.
The Body of Data:	Publish your research.

When preparing a presentation the first thing to determine is: *Who is your audience?* For instance, an overview of your implementation should be very different when there are different audiences. What you present to senior management may not be appropriate for the data center operational personnel, and what you say to the field test personnel won't be the same as your presentation to the application programmers.

The second thing to do in preparing your presentation is to *front load*! "Front loading" means getting directly to the "bottom line."

You do this by stating your conclusion(s) when you start your presentation. In business, unlike comedy, the punch line comes first. Studies show that an audience's attention diminishes appreciably over the course of a presentation. At the end, when the speaker says, "And in conclusion . . . " there is a little bump in retention. This is illustrated in Figure 3.1. So it's imperative that you "front load" and state your conclusions first.

After stating the "bottom line," you can then proceed to describe the method you used for your analysis (for example, you collected data that you compared to industry benchmarks, or you interviewed professionals in the field, or you stayed up late dreaming this stuff up, etc.). Finally, you write up your research with the correlating body of data and give it to the attendees. Presenters usually provide attendees with a copy of their slides or transparencies. However, it isn't a good idea to give a written report to the attendees until after your presentation; otherwise they will be reading the

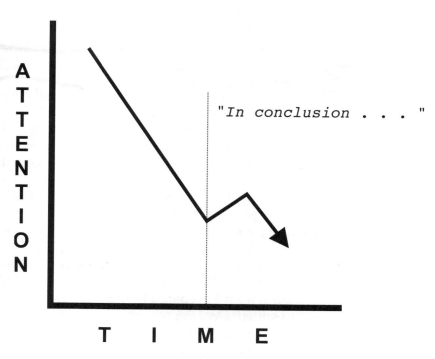

Figure 3.1. **Audience Attention Graph**

report while you're trying to speak and you won't hold their attention. Always put your name, phone number, and e-mail ID on the front of any reports or handouts so that anyone with questions can contact you at their discretion and convenience. Sometimes people don't want to ask their questions in front of an audience and would prefer to speak with you offline.

It's important to smile easily and often. Your expression and demeanor contributes greatly to the audience's receptivity to your material. Always be aware of the body language of your audience. Are people yawning, slouching, whispering, or looking bored? These are easy clues and they will suggest that you modify your presentation as you go along. Maybe it's time to ask for questions. When you do ask for questions, give the audience time to respond. Initially you will find that there are no questions! However, after the first few questions the dialogue between you and the audience will soon be rolling right along.

Try to make your presentation visual as well as verbal. Studies show that people retain only 10 percent of what they hear, 20 percent of what they see, but about 50 percent of what they both hear and see. Use flip charts, an overhead projector, a slide projector, or what have you. When using printed matter, vary the size and color of the fonts so everything doesn't look the same. And whatever you do, don't show one bullet chart after another; it really makes the audience go numb. Spice up your presentation with occasional graphics. The images can be relevant to the material, just plain silly, or both.

Be aware that anytime you rely on technological tools (overhead projector, slide projector, white board, etc.), there is a chance of something going amiss. So be prepared and check out your equipment and wiring before the presentation begins. It's amazing how many times people will start a presentation and then find that the projected image doesn't hit the screen, or the extension plug isn't long enough for the projector, or they don't know where or how to dim the lights. Don't let that happen to you.

To guide the logical flow of your presentation, use a note sheet or note cards that list the major topics you need to address. Don't read verbatim from a prepared text or from memorized material; it will sound stilted. Occasionally you can glance at your notes to remind yourself what you need to cover and where you are in the presentation. Another good method of covering your topic is to use an outline.

As an IC you're trying to bond with everyone, not set yourself apart, so don't place a podium or table between you and the audience. And most importantly, practice your presentation out loud by yourself. It's best to tape your presentation because then you can listen to it and determine your strengths and weaknesses. You'll also find out if the presentation is too long or too short. Then you can make appropriate adjustments.

Managing Process, Not Procedures

An effective IC manages the process, more than the procedures. Some Project Managers insist upon adhering strictly to the organization's project-management procedures, which ultimately can impact the system or product's implementation in a negative way. Managing the procedures doesn't always provide meaningful control of the implementation because the information generated could be misleading or, worst yet, incorrect. If a mistake is made in the design process, controlling the procedures often won't detect it, and the design flaw will be implemented. However, if you judiciously work the Joint Implementation Process you will have enough JIP Sessions for everyone to review and comment on every aspect of the implementation. It's difficult to implement a mistake when you manage the JIP process.

Seeking Feedback

Whether good or bad, you need feedback to learn. It's an invaluable reflection of yourself, although sometimes distorted by other people's biases. Since it's hard to determine someone's motivations for criticizing you, don't defend yourself when you get negative feedback, just acknowledge it and then try to learn from it. Be sure to ask for feedback because it is actually one of the few learning techniques available to an IC. Figure 3.2 is a symbolic representation of the feedback learning process.

COORDINATION

The IC understands the system because she attends every discussion about the product or its implementation. The IC maintains the Issues Log, so she takes part in resolving every issue. Therefore, the IC is able to coordinate all aspects of the implementation. ICs know

Figure 3.2.   Feedback Wheel

what the system or product to be implemented is all about, and which group is responsible for what. They also know which people are the experts about any given part of the implementation. So when the IC reviews each group's documentation, if something doesn't ring true or look right, she confers with the author of the document or consults with the resident expert on that issue. An IC can tell a lot from how someone writes a document. People who are clear and meticulous—detailing exactly what must be changed, and where those changes must be made—typically know what they are doing.

> *Organizations are learning that successful projects depend on co-ordination much more than any other single factor.*
>
> *—Peter Senge*

The One-Minute Rap

An IC should be able to explain the implementation and its objectives in one minute or less. Being able to quickly articulate the essence of your implementation is essential to its success. When soliciting support or "buy-in," people will expect you to quickly state your purpose. Many times you will encounter (in the elevator, the lunch line, or even on the phone) some person you have been trying to contact for weeks. This can be a "window of opportunity" to state your case, but you must do it succinctly. Almost invariably, the reason you've had trouble contacting this person is that she is very busy with her own agenda, and therefore loathe to give you the time to expound on the importance of your implementation. So you should have your one-minute "rap" prepared in advance, just in case an opportunity to speak with her unexpectedly presents itself.

Preparing your rap is no easy task. Sometimes it can take weeks to fully understand your implementation and its ramifications. Without this understanding, you can't prepare a comprehensive yet concise rap. One effective technique for understanding your implementation is to *listen* to what you say when discussing the implementation with friends and colleagues. Try taping what you say when you make presentations that concern the implementation. By *listening* to what you say in conversations, and on tape, you will begin to grok the essence of the implementation. Then practice your rap aloud, and time yourself. Although this preparation will take time, it will all be worth it when you make that encounter and know exactly what to say. Otherwise you'll end up blowing the exchange and lying in bed at night thinking, "If only I had said . . ." or "I should have made the point that . . ."

Global View

As the IC, you must discover and understand the "big picture," and then communicate your enlightened view to the implementation participants, whose viewpoints will necessarily be more compartmentalized than yours. However, people often think they know all about the implementation, only to find out later—and sometimes unpleasantly—that there are whole areas with which they are unfamiliar. This can have disruptive consequences, and so it is up to the IC to prevent this. For example, another project could be testing at the same time as your implementation team, and making changes

in the same source code so as to negate the validity of your team's testing milestones.

Wandering Around

To paraphrase Tom Peters (who co-opted the phrase from Hewlett Packard), "wandering around" is the way the IC gathers vital information. You need to know who's going to "shoot you down" and who you can count on at crunch time. You do this by literally and figuratively moving around the organization, constantly building the working relationships necessary to coordinate the implementation, and establishing a network of informants who can tell you what is happening "in the trenches." It might seem like pointless rambling, but wandering around is actually important work. However, because it might appear like wasting time or sandbagging to some, be prepared to defend what you're doing if questioned. Just as a writer does important work by leaning back and wandering around in her daydreams for ideas, in the same way the IC does important work wandering around to gather information and build support for the implementation.

Impacting Others

You have to find out who is impacted by your implementation, and then make sure they know about it. Don't expect them to knock on your door and say, "Oh please tell me what I need to know." Typically, people impacted by the implementation don't want to be bothered by the news. So the IC has to bug them and say, "You're really gonna have to listen to me because I'm gonna affect your application."

> Once upon an implementation, a certain group within the organization was going to be dramatically impacted by the implementation. Despite heroic efforts by the IC to pester and cajole this group, they didn't want to participate in her implementation or even pay attention to her. Then at the "eleventh hour" this group finally realized what the implementation was going to mean to their application, and they went "ballistic." The IC was in good shape because she had kept her Project Manager apprised, and had documented this group's intransigence in her reports. Fortunately, she also had the foresight to prepare in advance all the documentation this group required to integrate with the implementation.

The IC as Supplier of Information

The IC actively and deliberately works to increase everyone's knowledge of the system or product to be implemented, and also expands their awareness of the organization itself. By being informed and aware, the implementation participants can make sound business decisions. The IC processes information by converting the reams of data she receives and elicits every day into usable information. By interpreting and reconstituting project news and data, the IC regularly produces information that increases the implementation participant's knowledge and/or expands their awareness.

> *Information gathering is the basis of all other managerial work, which is why I choose to spend so much of my day doing it.*
>
> *—Andrew Grove*

Proactivity

ICs are "proactive" and *make it easy for people* by being totally accommodating. The IC tries to provide all the information everyone will need before they ask for it. You should try to provide anything that is requested, without question or hesitation. By accommodating everyone you foster reciprocity so that others will be accommodating toward you.

ICs try not to compromise or circumvent the standards and procedures of the organization just so the implementation can realize its objectives. ICs try to anticipate problems with standards or procedures and then take the proactive role of working with the policymakers to improve or modify those standards and procedures.

Vendor Relationships

ICs sometimes encounter Project Managers or even entire organizations that have "lousy relationships" with vendors. One of the first things the IC must do is improve these relationships. Otherwise it's much more difficult to solve problems involving the vendors' products or services. For example, if a system crashes, the vendors could ask, "Did you test all your interfaces? Did you test all your communication lines?" This kind of second-guessing is divisive and counterproductive. You want the vendors to jump right in and help you with the problem. So it's important to place priority on building strong relationships with all the vendors whose products are part of the implementation. This, too, is part of wandering around and fencebuilding.

Selling Success

The IC needs to promote to everyone the overall value of a successful implementation. You do this by getting the participants to identify with the *stakeholders* of the organization (i.e., the owners, the shareholders, the taxpayers, etc.) because their influence crosses many divisional boundaries. The stakeholders have funded the organization, so everyone working on the implementation holds their trust and operates at their behest.

The IC pragmatically recognizes that people will do whatever is in their own best interests. Therefore, the burden falls on the IC to persuade people that supporting the implementation is good for them. The IC must sell the participants on the concept that the implementation's goal or mission is bigger than anyone else's. In the final analysis, everyone works for the stakeholders; not their boss, or their boss's boss, etc. For the stakeholders, this system or product makes sense and so the implementation needs to get done.

Even if an individual or a group or groups may be negatively impacted, this system or product must be implemented because it benefits the stakeholders, who count most.

The Importance of Brevity

To be successful, the IC demonstrates a tremendous respect for a professional's time. In a presentation at which many of the attendees have heard you speak about the implementation before, say something like "Some of you have already seen this pitch, or don't need to know that much about it, so I'll just give you the basics. On the front of this hand-out is my name and phone number. If you want to know more, please call." Then present the minimal information: who you are, what you're planning, and when you're going to do it. The IC usually hands out useful documents at every presentation and at most JIP Sessions. This gives the participants something to carry back to their desks with the IC's name, phone number, e-mail ID, and organization mail-stop. Then the participants can contact you at their convenience.

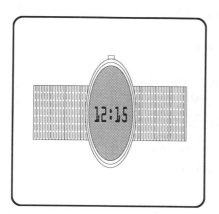

Point of Contact

When coordinating an implementation, the IC ideally wants to deal with a single person who has the responsibility for integrating all issues relevant to a particular system, application, group, team, etc. The IC's nightmare comes true when the person who represents

Need point of contact for each dept.

this "point of contact" keeps changing. It's impossible to negotiate agreements and commitments if you never deal with the same person twice. Without agreements and commitments on which you can rely, you will never effectively coordinate an implementation. Therefore, if the person responsible for a particular point of contact keeps changing, you need to escalate the issue, so that management will designate a fixed point of contact.

FACILITATION

A good facilitator can direct a meeting without knowing much about the subject matter being discussed. However, facilitating as an IC is different than the traditional role of the facilitator. ICs are field-experienced practitioners who know information systems, know how and when to ask the right questions, and know when something sounds not right or even bizarre.

The complexity of information systems demands a specialized facilitator. Professionals in our industry cannot trust someone who doesn't understand information systems to direct important JIP Sessions. As the facilitator, you need to know what the JIP Session participants are trying to accomplish technologically.

Facilitation Guidelines

1. Be Prepared.
2. Be energetic; show enthusiasm!
3. Respect professionals' time.
4. Promote peer-to-peer interaction.
5. Empathize with the group.
6. Don't defend yourself when criticized.
7. Praise the group for its work.

Making JIP Sessions Open

A typical attitude problem that ICs encounter is when a manager says to the programmers, "My job is to plan and manage. Your job is to do the programming." This dictum turns everyone off, and rightly so. An effective IC therefore solicits everyone's comments at every JIP Session—not just communicating with those who are "important." You should stress the open nature of the session by inquiring, "Does anyone have any worries or concerns about any aspect of the implementation? Would anyone like to share their thoughts in the shower today—about the implementation, that is? If you think of *anything* in the coming weeks, please call me."

Normally people don't expect the IC—who is in a power position—to bring this kind of freedom to the JIP Session. Opening the JIP Session to everyone's comments is a powerful technique because it allows a tremendous amount of good information to bubble up from the bottom that would never trickle down from the top.

Directness

Directness is an asset; it works better if you call a system failure a "crash" instead of the "unavailability of system resources due to operational objectives not being realized at this time." An example of directness being crucial is when a technical specialist puts either limitations or constraints on a deliverable to the extent that it becomes a major issue. The IC must understand the technological implications and be able to say, "Gee, that doesn't sound right to me." Then the IC can judiciously steer the dialogue toward a reasonable technological solution. The IC always strives to cooperatively prevent the implementation from getting derailed by anyone's inappropriate dictates.

> Once upon an implementation, the IC had a situation in which a Database Administrator (DBA) stated that after a certain date no one would have access to specific tables in the database. The IC immediately realized this inaccessibility would greatly impede every application's testing. By understanding the technological issues (such as that the security package controls access to the tables while the data base management software controls access to specific fields in the tables), the IC directly pointed this out to the DBA and got her to modify her position. The testing was able to proceed as planned.

Getting Unstuck

An IC should know how to help a group when it "gets stuck." First, you need to realize that the group either ran out of new ideas, or is obstructed by some logical or physical impediment. You may have to rely on your intuition, because it isn't always evident that such problems exist. Try to be creative and use a salesperson's touch to get the group back on track.

When dealing with a particularly tough sales call, the founder of ASK, Sandra Kurtzig, says her idea is to keep poking until she hits something that works. ICs go at the group in the same way. "Come on, folks. Let's try this. Let's try that. But let's keep trying." They creatively keep plugging away until they get the group unstuck and moving in a positive direction.

Facilitating a Transformation

Through their facilitation and orchestration skills, ICs can transform JIP Session participants from a collection of diverse personalities with divergent agendas into a creative, coordinated social organism. When such a transformation occurs, the participants speak of how the JIP Session "just flew by," when in fact it may have taken four or five hours. ICs get jazzed when they facilitate this transformation, and it also feels good to everyone in the JIP Session.

Being Specific

ICs always insist on people being specific and getting down to essential facts. You should always be asking, "Who said that? When did they say it?" When someone makes a vague or offhand comment such as, "Oh, that will never work," you should come right back by asking, "What do you specifically mean by saying that?" If they try to skew responsibility or justification to someone not in the JIP Session, you should stay on the case by asking, "How can I check this with that person?" As an IC you don't ever want anything to slide. You want specifics.

The Agenda

ICs learn to live according to the lists of things that need to get done in JIP Sessions and even in personal interactions. This is their *agenda*. When facilitating a JIP Session the necessity of having an agenda is evident, but ICs also develop agendas for use in calling someone on the phone. The importance of enumerating what you need to discuss, either at large in a JIP Session or one-on-one with an individual, is not to be minimized. Without an agenda you will invariably find yourself later saying, "Gosh, I should have asked them about . . ." or "Darn, I forgot to mention . . ." Figure 3.3 is an example of an agenda an IC would jot down for an interview.

Agenda for Interview with Cheryl West

1 Find out what Cheryl expects
   of the system to be implemented
2 When will Cheryl be ready to
   commit resources to the implementation?
3 Share my concerns & find out about
   Cheryl's concerns
4 What's the source of tension between
   Cheryl & Tom Jones - can it be resolved?
5 Will the other implementations in Cheryl's
   area conflict with this implementation?
6 Are there any synchronization issues between
   the other systems in Cheryl's area & this
   implementation?
7 Appraise Cheryl of this implementation's
   projected schedule & deliverables

Figure 3.3. **An Agenda**

ICs always have an agenda regarding what needs to be accomplished in every JIP Session, and they make sure that the group keeps moving from item to item. As the IC, you don't want to run out of time for that JIP Session and find that the group is still on item two of a twelve-item agenda. Since you don't want the group to waste valuable time on trifling or peripheral issues, you need to see to it that most of the items on your agenda are at least addressed if not resolved. However, if a significant issue is raised that isn't on the agenda, make sure you put it on the Issues Log and then deal with it as part of the agenda for the next JIP Session.

Cutting Someone Off

There are so many logistical issues in every JIP Session that the IC must decide when someone has spoken too long, and then be able to cut them off. Determine how long you should let someone go on by assessing their digression with regard to the JIP Session's goal(s). When you think it's time, interrupt and truthfully say something like, "We aren't here to solve every problem. We need to get on with today's JIP Session. So what we need to do with this discussion is to describe the problem, enter it into the Issues Log, and identify who the group thinks are the right people to work on it. And then let's move to the next item on the agenda."

Fielding Dumb Questions

Everyone prefers to ignore "dumb questions." However, many times the questions merely sound stupid because the querist "isn't even in the ballpark" and doesn't understand what the implemen-

> Once upon an implementation, the person representing the business operations in a JIP Session kept harping, "Where's the balancing? How do we balance?" The IC's initial reaction was to think, "Buzz-off, balancing is an accounting activity we can deal with later." But after the IC opened the discussion to the question of balancing, it turned out that the accounting issues were keeping the operational areas from supporting the implementation. Not understanding how the balancing was going to work, the operations groups balked, and without their support the implementation wasn't even going to get out of the planning stage.

tation is all about. Your instinctive reaction is to shake your head and try to get these people out of your hair. But imagine yourself in their position—having something to offer but being misunderstood and looking foolish. Don't cut yourself off from what could be valid or important information. Addressing and answering even dumb questions effectively overcomes resistance to a system or product's implementation.

Respecting a Professional's Time

One of the key elements in conducting successful JIP Sessions deals with showing tremendous respect for the time of the professionals you have asked to attend. This point can't be stressed too strongly. Professionals, especially technical specialists, don't enjoy meetings because they usually have so much other work to do. You have to demonstrate that their presence is valued by addressing those issues that necessitated their attendance and then letting them go promptly after their contribution. You are courting doom if you conduct your JIP Sessions as a death march intent on resolving a problem that has no relevance to most of the participants. One way of defeating the doom patrol is to release those participants who were required to attend just because the problem happens to be in their area or group, but who have nothing specific to learn or contribute.

You can make sure you aren't wasting professionals' time by taking a straw poll at the start of the JIP Session about the items to be addressed. The responses should tell you whether these are the items of concern, and whether you're duplicating someone else's effort. Try not to abuse the JIP Session time-constraints by permitting lengthy digressions. JIP Sessions tend to be populated with technical specialists who hate meetings and only grudgingly give you their time.

Always assume you are dealing with top-notch people who clearly have something of value to contribute to the implementation. Why else would you have them there in the JIP Session? To facilitate their contribution, make the JIP Session comfortable for them and give them the respect they deserve. ICs tend to be in the position of begging for people's time because they typically don't have authority over anyone. If the IC doesn't treat everyone's time as a valuable commodity, she won't be able to get anyone to help her with the implementation. If you waste people's time, the word will get around the organization and you will lose credibility. After that, it will only become harder to get people to attend the JIP Sessions.

Shared Understanding

At many JIP Sessions the IC must deal with the reality that the participants have different knowledge levels about an issue. It's imperative to the success of the JIP Session that these differences be equalized so that the group has a "shared understanding" of what the implementation is supposed to accomplish. ICs typically rely on the person in the JIP Session who is most knowledgeable on a particular subject to make a presentation and bring everyone up to speed. As the IC you shouldn't be making all the presentations.

Shared Responsibility

The preferred strategy for getting the participants to accept responsibility for the JIP Session is to let them make the decisions. When the participants ask, "Is this JIP Session over?" the IC responds, "Well, are we done? Have we covered everything we needed to cover?" Let them tell you. Asking questions creates a "shared responsibility" between the IC and the JIP Session participants, and also amongst the participants themselves.

ICs Always Ask the Participants Questions Such As:

1. Have we stated this issue correctly?
2. Can we go on to the next topic?
3. Here's what I think we just said. Did I get it right?

4. What do we think about this?
5. Do we have time to cover this or do we need another JIP Session?

Fostering Cooperation

It's critical that all the groups involved in an implementation cooperate. The IC's responsibility is to get all the disparate technological systems and personnel to communicate with one another. What was once a single discussion between the business users and the systems developers in a homogeneous environment is now broken into many discussions between the many divisions of the organization's systems and personnel in the heterogeneous environments of today. At each interface of systems and personnel, assumptions can confuse and confound, or information can be misunderstood. Communication can get weird between the business users and the systems people. Cooperation now is paramount because implementations can quickly get ugly in multi-platform, distributed environments where there are more crevices for issues to fall into.

> Once upon an implementation, the IC found herself unable to get an acceptable level of cooperation during a JIP Session. Her reaction was to just keep poking at it. She asked, "How can we resolve this issue?" to which someone responded, "You don't want to solve that problem. You want to solve this other problem that I've been trying to solve for years and have gotten nowhere." The IC was not deterred. She came right back and said, "Yeah, well if I had to resolve *this* issue, what should I do?" Knowing that every implementation is a collaborative effort by all parties, she was not dissuaded from pushing for cooperation in order to achieve success.

Resolving Objections

When an idea or proposal is presented in a JIP Session the IC must be prepared to handle any objections, and then translate these objections into resolutions. Professionals in the information systems industry are typically very bright and they can dream up objections that can sound very real and very new. However, ICs find that those persons who voice objections will suggest the solutions themselves if their objections are handled appropriately. A programmer will say, "How are you going to handle the reversals of the reversals?" To which the IC responds, "I don't know, we haven't thought about that yet. What do you think we ought to do?" The key is to acknowledge the objection as real, and then *turn it back* to the person or group for a resolution. ICs don't take it upon themselves to solve every problem. The participants in the JIP Session are usually better qualified to resolve the objections. The group can clarify the objections and, when necessary, point the IC to the people they should talk to for a resolution. There are *lots* of these kinds of discussions in every JIP Session.

Handling Egos

Some people in all professions have big egos. Professionals in information systems with big egos come to JIP Sessions puffed up with their own agendas, issues, and personal concerns. However, ICs invariably find that these people are willing to set aside any ego issues when they sense that the IC intends to get real work done in the JIP Session. The IC sets the tone by promulgating an attitude of "Let's get on with it and get our work done." In this environment everyone in the JIP Session quickly gets the idea that being professional is where it's at. No one wants to be the only egomaniac in a room full of pros.

Voicing Concerns

The IC should continually encourage everyone to voice their concerns in JIP Sessions. Sometimes this can be annoying but ICs find that people voicing a concern usually have a good point (although that may not be evident at the time). By raising their concerns these people help the group achieve a more comprehensive solution. So don't let the JIP Session participants squelch valid concerns.

On the other hand, some concerns are merely personal complaints that can become divisive to the group if permitted to continue. For instance, one IC was facilitating a JIP Session at which someone kept whining about having to be there. The IC dealt with this by asking the participants, "Does anyone have any issues for Winnie's group? Is there anyone who would object to her leaving?" No one said anything so the IC excused this person from the JIP Session. She had a hard time leaving the room because what Winnie really wanted to do was whine some more.

Establishing a Comfort Level

The IC uses orchestration skills to help the group focus its energies upon the task at hand. The IC periodically verifies that everyone feels comfortable with the decisions being made. This is the so-called "comfort level" within the JIP Session. If some aspect of an issue hasn't been covered, someone in the JIP Session is still going to have a problem. So the IC says, "Is everyone OK with us moving off this issue? Have we covered every aspect?" This gives that someone yet another chance to say, "You know, I'm not really sure how we're going to do this." You get a sense of when people are thinking and churning, and not really ready to move on. Giving them the opportunity to voice their concerns and receive feedback makes everyone more ready when you do go on.

Having Strong Opinions

ICs differ from the traditional model of a facilitator because they have *strong opinions* and they *voice* them. As a generalization, you should let the participants find the solutions themselves; most of your own ideas will eventually be suggested within the group anyway. However, if the group is bogged down on a certain point, the IC should say, "Why don't we do it this way?" Of course the group may point out the flaws in that alternative, but the intention is to

Once upon an implementation, while facilitating a JIP Implementation Planning Session, an outspoken IC was approached at the break by the Project Manager, who said, "I want to caution you about stepping out of your role as the JIP Session facilitator by stating an opinion. You are not being neutral!" The IC responded, "You bet! This group needs my input." The IC pointed out that she knew what she was doing; her bias was intentional. The group was a collection of neophyte users who knew little about information systems and desperately needed some expert direction. After all, implementing information systems is a complicated, knowledge-based process. You can't expect the people in a two-day JIP Session to resolve all the issues without some professional expertise. Several times during the JIP Session the group had skewed into such irrelevant tangents that the IC needed to step forward and impart information about basic industry standards.

keep the dialogue moving. The IC should present strong opinions, but just as readily be able to change or get off them. Do not get attached to your own opinions. If someone has a better suggestion, you should wholeheartedly support it. The IC works for results, not personal aggrandizement.

Backing Off

Even though the IC is supposed to be in control of the JIP Session, sometimes it's best to just "back off" and let people talk. The other participants may wonder, "What is the IC doing? Why doesn't she make them stop talking?" But sometimes there is real communication going on between several people, which could prove important to the implementation. So the IC lets them take the initiative for awhile and then says, "OK, here's what I think you folks just worked out between yourselves." Then try to summarize the discussion on the Session Boards. Always be sure to ask, "Is that right? Did I cover everything?"

Giving Space

It's important to give JIP-Session participants "space" to properly compose their responses. Sometimes that space is silence, during which they think through their answer. Don't always expect an immediate response. Also, you shouldn't pose a question and then answer it yourself. It's a great temptation to answer your own questions, but the trick is to put the questions to the group. ICs invariably find that the people in a JIP Session represent an overflowing reservoir of knowledge and creativity, and can answer most questions themselves.

INTERACTION

Common courtesy is an important attribute for a successful IC. Returning calls and answering correspondence promptly are courtesies that build the IC's credibility within any organization. Therefore, be sincere in your interactions. Don't say to someone, "Let's do lunch" if you have no intention of ever meeting with that person. In your role as a coordinator and builder of human networks within the organization, your personal integrity is your primary asset, and should not be compromised.

Treat every person with the attention and respect you expect to receive yourself. Don't fawn over superiors; to be effective you need to be viewed as an equal. Don't be insensitive to entry-level personnel; everyone within the organization is a source of information that can be of value.

Telephone Conversations

When calling people, you never know what problems or time constraints they might be dealing with. Therefore, after your greeting it's always good to preface any dialogue with the question, "Is this a good time to talk?" Extending this courtesy lets the other person know you're sensitive to her situation and respect her time. She'll let you know if it's a good time to proceed with the conversation.

Breaking Appointments

As the implementation's coordinator, you will make many appointments, and also break a lot of them. It's best if you have *verbal confirmation* from the person involved before rolling any appointment off your calendar. Sending voice mail, e-mail, or inter-office mail is not sufficient. Only by speaking with someone can you make sure there are no misunderstandings.

Noticing Workstyles

Be aware of and take the time to notice everyone's individual workstyle.

Ask Yourself These Questions:

1. What is their point of view?
2. What are their priorities?
3. What's the best medium to use to contact them?

The answers to these questions give you some sense of each person's workstyle, and then you can adjust your interaction appropriately. For example, some people only use one form of communication. If you know that's all they review daily, you can focus on that medium. Conversely, for other people, you know that your only hope of communicating with them is the wide-spectrum approach of hitting them with everything you've got. So you send them voice mail, e-mail, and inter-office mail—and then you go across the street and up twenty floors to pin a note on their chair!

Exerting Leverage

Leverage is the ability to bring pressure to bear on someone or something. When some person or group is unresponsive to the needs of the implementation, you may need to escalate the issue or otherwise try to exert leverage to bring about the action required. Unfortunately, this isn't always possible.

When you can't get leverage through escalation, then it's time to look for someone else to do the work—and *reduce your dependency* on that group. If you poke on a jellyfish for awhile you realize it

Once upon an implementation, a participating group produced a sloppy JIP Interface-Design-Specification Document that was not only incomplete but contained a major misunderstanding about the implementation. Rather than sit down with the group and tell them their document was from Podunk, the IC called a JIP Session that included people with a thorough knowledge of the implementation. At the JIP Session, the experts went through the document and pointed out what had to be changed, corrected, and/or added. At the end of the session the IC asked, "OK, when can we expect to see the updated document?" The group's representative answered, "Well, we're not going to update this JIP Interface-Design-Specification document now. We'll wait until my group gets down our work queue to your implementation, then we'll pull it off the shelf and update it at that time." This is where *leverage* is needed to get this group in step with the implementation, because it just isn't good business practice to dangle on some unspecified future date for correct documentation. The IC escalated the issue to the group's manager, saying, "Am I confused or just confounded that your group is unwilling to correct their JIP Interface-Design-Specification Document? This seems flaky because this document will be used to place my implementation in your work queue. It would seem prudent to make it accurate now, wouldn't you say?" Regrettably, the IC only got some waffley answers that defended the group's process rather than addressing the IC's concerns. Sometimes a group is more dedicated to their domain's priorities than to the IC's implementation.

isn't going to move just because you're poking it. That's when you know it's time to go around it.

Using Persuasion

There are situations in which the IC has no leverage and needs to persuade other groups in the organization to support her implementation. For example, there are business users who don't own any data, don't own the business systems, don't have any programmers on their staff, and yet are still responsible for the implementation of a product. In these situations persuasion is paramount. This is where all the basic IC skills (facilitating, networking, building relationships, being accommodating, etc.) are brought to bear. You need to do all the work, be the most accommodating party, and make sure that everyone else is happy.

Being Persistent

Persistence is the thread that finally gets a system or product implementation sewn up. For example, without persistence you may find that it's impossible to make contact with certain important people, and that may have potentially serious consequences for your implementation. ICs have been known to stand outside the person's office and wait for them to show up in the morning. It's important to remember that when you finally do encounter the person *do not mention* the fact that they have not returned any of your calls or correspondence. Just state your case as succinctly as possible. ICs are always courteous and they are equally persistent. They will not be dissuaded from their objectives by someone who is either ignoring or hiding from them.

Testing Perceptions

The satisfaction levels of the implementation's participants directly correlate with the implementation's success. You need to keep "testing the waters" about whether people are satisfied with the implementation process at every point. The feedback you receive can tip you off to issues you may be missing.

ICs Always Ask Questions Such As:

1. Has the other application group handed over their work to you yet?
2. Are you *satisfied* with what you got?
3. What did you expect that you didn't receive?

Many problems, and particularly the perceptions of these problems, are conditioned by personality conflicts, political problems, or someone feeling that they lack the authority to ask questions. In the latter case, the IC can ask, "Is it OK if I ask this for you?"

Satisfaction is an emotional, not a logical experience.

—*Barry Posner*

Test your own perceptions of a situation or person by comparing them with those of other professionals whose judgment you trust and whose perspectives differ from your own. Being human, you can make judgments about a person or situation that could easily be wrong. But if your perceptions about some group's intransigence are confirmed, then you know it's time to either apply leverage or *reduce your dependency* on that group.

A Sense of Humor

ICs find that displaying a sense of humor is an excellent communication device. Studies show that people who laugh easily, and can make others laugh with them, tend to be more creative, less rigid, and more willing to consider and embrace new ideas and methods. An IC needs to possess all these attributes to be successful.

About Networking

Networking and building relationships create the foundation for getting work done. Without a network of relationships you will never be able to successfully coordinate an implementation. If a relationship with a key person needs to be developed, taking her to lunch is a good medium. *Note*: Drinks after work are more or less passé; many people don't drink alcohol or smoke cigarettes anymore, and the "beery" ambiance of a bar can be less effective than that of a charming restaurant or popular coffeehouse.

ASSUMING AUTHORITY

A common lament heard from people trying to coordinate some aspect of a project is, "I have no power." This expresses the classic dilemma of having responsibility without command. Since organizations still carry the vestiges of a hierarchy, many times people will assume they can't get authority because their position doesn't warrant it. However, oftentimes one can *assume authority* on one's own initiative. In fact, if it's done judiciously, ICs have found that implementation personnel love it. Everyone hates a vacuum of authority whether they admit it or not. When an IC is confronted by an authority vacuum, she should take command just to make sure there is a leader. Most people are so busy keeping their own jobs afloat that they can't possibly provide all the direction an implementation requires.

So now you've stepped forward and taken a commanding role. However, assumption of authority requires a certain amount of treading on toes, and you will hear some complaints about that. Your response should make the Project Manager and implementation participants understand that you're not ego-tripping or politicking under the table—you're trying to get the system implemented. Tell them, "Shucks, we all need to get this job done and here's what we need to be doing right now. Thanks for your cooperation!"

About Escalating

Escalation, or resorting to higher authority, is considered a corporate bugbear. However, it's a major leveraging tool within any organization. If the Project Manager and IC find they aren't getting support from one level of management, then either or both can intrepidly "go upstairs" to the next level. There they can say things like, "We thought we had a commitment from you guys for our implementation. Now so-and-so in your subgroup says she can't possibly attend the JIP Sessions. Is there a problem, or does she need to be reminded of priorities?" Usually the manager will say, "Oh, I'm sorry—we really support your implementation; that person will be at your next JIP Session." If that person still doesn't show up as promised, then you escalate again to a higher level in the organization. When escalating, ICs generally find that higher-level managers accept responsibility more readily than middle-level managers.

If a key person doesn't attend a JIP Session, everyone's time has been wasted. The IC therefore takes responsibility for informing higher management that a problem exists (lack of attendance). An uncooperative senior manager may unwittingly solve your problem by saying, "Your implementation is NOT our priority"—which gives you political ammunition to go to your Project Manager and say, "This manager says the implementation is not their priority and here's how it's going to slow your implementation schedule." Your Project Manager can then decide how to proceed. Obviously, the Project Manager can and probably will escalate the issue, but with more clout than you.

Working the Management Team

ICs believe in "working" the management team. Some people call this escalation and therefore avoid it. However, it's important to keep senior management (in addition to the Project Manager) informed about who is and who is not contributing to the implementation effort. Senior management might be able to make some changes, such as reassigning a particular task or area of responsibility, or directing the appropriate people to place a higher priority on your implementation.

Management Commitment

Implementations need a commitment by a senior manager in the organization to be successful. If your implementation lacks management commitment, then you and your Project Manager should escalate your implementation and its issues to the requisite level of management. What level of manager you require is determined by the importance and impact of the system or product to be implemented. Which manager you should approach is determined by the sales axiom: "Who's making the buy?" Many times it isn't evident who's in control of the budget and making the "go or no go" decision. Usually the decision maker is not the Project Manager. To be successful you need to figure out who the decision maker is.

> *Many times salespeople find themselves losing a sale because they failed to locate or speak to the <u>real decision maker</u>.*
>
> —*Robert Miller and Steven Heiman*

Gaining Sponsorship

The sponsor is the manager (typically someone senior in the organization) who is accountable for the project of which your implementation is a part. The way you interact with the project's sponsor can determine the success of your implementation. Full disclosure is important. Don't protect or shield the sponsor from what is happening regarding the implementation. Don't do the sponsor's job by returning her calls or writing her correspondence. For an implementation to succeed, the sponsor must actively participate; otherwise you effectively have no sponsor.

Don't get isolated by letting the sponsor tell you, "The Implementation Plan looks good. Go do it (yourself)." You can counteract this situation with two techniques. First, assign tasks to the sponsor as part of the Implementation Plan. This keeps her involved. Second, when you find issues that can't be resolved at the operational or middle management levels, then with the Project Manager's OK, escalate these issues to the sponsor's attention. Accountability not only flows down but *up* the managerial hierarchy, and escalation is the best way to keep the sponsor responsible for her dictates. She must make decisions or the implementation won't go forward. You can say, "Our implementation is priority five for this group and they say they've never gotten past priority three. Do you want this group to support the implementation?" If the sponsor makes no move on the issue (in effect dumping the problem back on you) then it's time for you and the Project Manager to start looking for another sponsor, a co-sponsor, or even a champion for that particular issue. Usually you will find that the sponsor is grateful to you for bringing critical issues to her attention and is also supportive of your efforts.

If your implementation is one that the organization doesn't want badly enough for its senior management to sponsor, support, and sign-off, then it's time to look for another assignment. Try not to get even peripherally involved with an implementation that lacks a legitimate sponsor. Also, be aware that situations happen in which an IC gets assigned to an implementation that initially has an excellent sponsor. So excellent, in fact, that midway through the implementation, the sponsor gets moved (for example, to a sick division in an attempt to save it). Then the IC's implementation is reassigned to a new manager who doesn't understand the need for active sponsorship, and the implementation withers away.

Usually, the ideas that ICs try to implement are those of the Project Manager's, not their own. However, it is possible that you may be implementing your own ideas. Either way, understanding what sponsorship means, knowing how to involve your sponsor, and what to expect is crucial to your implementation's success.

The Vision Thing

The project and implementation's sponsor provides the direction, vision, and grasp of issues that make the business run. If the sponsor backs off and just lets the implementation float along, then the project goes into a degenerative situation. When a project and the implementation loses it's vision, lots of good ideas float around and collide with each other. Without vision nobody knows which ones to spend time on. An implementation needs a leader who says, "This is what's important."

All implementation strategies are written for a sponsor who already has a vision in mind. Therefore, you can't go off on a tangent. Since you want the sponsor to agree to your Implementation Plan, you have to sanitize and filter what you submit for approval so it's in line with her vision. You may even have to negotiate with the sponsor to get your strategy accepted.

If your implementation lacks vision, you can try to reconstitute the project into something useful by using the techniques of escalation, assuming authority, seeking consensus through JIP Sessions, etc. However, ICs have experienced limited success in their attempts at reconstituting projects that don't have strong input from a sponsor.

Dealing with Gurus

Gurus are key resource personnel who have internalized a lot of critical information. These people are usually so valuable that it's almost impossible to get any of their time. They are sometimes whiz-kid technical types who've never had to document the functionality of their area of responsibility. Gurus have even been known to resist documentation for fear of losing control. However, the IC and the Project Manager cannot be held hostage to these technicians.

Gurus often embody a style of working and thinking that is too quick for written communication. If they aren't disciplined, or lack experience at documenting their area of responsibility (in a form others can understand), then they are not going to do it well. And, they'll be defensive. To document the guru's knowledge the IC should offer to interview her about her area, write up the meeting, and have the guru review the conversation in the form of hardcopy. The IC sometimes has to make the offer several times before the guru will act on it. It's an iterative process: interviews, documentation, reviewing the hardcopy for inconsistencies and omissions, further conversations, more documentation, and more reviews. This process can be frustrating and even humiliating because the guru will say, "No, you have this wrong, you misunderstood that, and so forth." Notwithstanding the difficulties, a document must be produced that captures the guru's body of knowledge for all to review.

The IC can really help the implementation by slugging it out with the guru until proper documentation has been produced. The IC strives to make the guru's technical knowledge into a subset of the business knowledge of both the IC and the Project Manager. It can be really difficult working with a guru to build a document but well worth it because the documentation always moves the implementation forward. When documented, the guru's knowledge helps to create a disciplined approach to the work being done, and the implementation is likely to have fewer problems.

Gurus can be the bane of the IC's effort for a systematic implementation. Some gurus want to "run and gun," but as an IC you want to eliminate those kinds of work habits. A guru actually remarked to the IC who was coordinating a very large, complicated, and high-risk implementation, "Man alive, it's getting hard for me to improvise this anymore." Hopefully, when the gurus realize they're in over their heads and can't improvise, they will seek your assistance.

Gurus have been known to willfully withhold information. Some have even held competitions to see who could miss the most JIP Sessions. ICs cannot tolerate this kind of behavior. By using such techniques as documenting the guru's knowledge, applying pressure via escalation, and reducing dependency, an IC can live with, or at least survive, the organization's most reticent gurus.

Once upon an implementation, the IC worked with a particularly vexing guru who, whenever confronted with a problem report, would say, "Oh, don't worry, we weren't testing that function anyway," or "I already fixed that and it won't happen again." However, the IC was not intimidated into accepting the guru's OK with regard to these problems. The IC documented everything the guru did and said. This way she was able to substantiate the problems with hardcopy and justify the actions she took. If the IC had just gone along with the guru's excuses, she would have been in some trouble, left "holding the bag" for the guru.

ICs often find that the gurus who solve all the problems are also the same folks who create other problems with their haphazard

"I-can-fix-anything" attitude. While most people would agree that every project flies on the wings of talent, it's still important to find ways to work with (and when necessary, work around) the gurus.

IMPLEMENTATION ISSUES

ICs know that taking care of the numerous, unremitting issues that can develop into problems is essential to the success of every implementation. ICs don't wait for these issues to develop into problems, because by that time it may be too late to effect any solution.

> *You must find the implementation's problems before they find you.*
>
> *—IC's Truism*

Issue Resolution

The IC lets everyone know at every JIP Session that as the owner of the Issues Log (described in Chapter 4) she is responsible for seeing that issues are identified, and she is then going to *work the issues*, if necessary escalate the issues, and ultimately resolve the issues. After an issue is identified and logged, the person or group who raised the issue is usually its de facto owner. However, the JIP Session participants should discuss whether that person or group should in fact own the issue. Sometimes the issue should belong to some other person or group even though they didn't bring it to everyone's attention. So the "rightful owner" of the issue needs to be identified. Then the JIP Session participants should determine if anyone else needs to be notified and perhaps be invited to the next JIP Session at which that issue will be discussed. Since an issue by definition is "in dispute or unresolved," it usually takes some work by the IC and at least two JIP Sessions to resolve it.

Issue Resolution

1. What is the issue?
2. Who currently owns the issue?
3. Who should own the issue?
4. Who does the IC need to notify?
5. Who does the IC need to invite to the JIP Session?

To be successful, an IC must sometimes turn to escalation as the only avenue for issue resolution. Escalation is needed when—as often happens— an issue can't be resolved because the right people are not being notified. Sometimes organizational personnel feel intimidated when it comes to approaching a senior manager to discuss a problem. But if the problem belongs to that senior manager you won't get resolution until you escalate the problem to their attention! Don't procrastinate, escalate!

> Once upon an implementation, the IC worked in an organization in which the unspoken rule was that if you raised the issue then you had to have the answer. Without the solution, you weren't supposed to raise the issue. That particular organizational culture effectively denigrated people who raised issues. Therefore, the IC could never identify the issues and find out who was responsible for them. Sometimes it seemed to the IC that the only way to possibly identify and determine responsibility for the issues would be to call the entire division into a JIP Session. But how could she get a thousand people into one room? No managerial techniques or sage advice could help her with this impossible situation. The IC's implementation ground on without issues getting identified or resolved and consequently nothing ever got installed. The IC also found out that the project had experienced a succession of managers: they didn't stay with the implementation effort because they declined to be party to a nightmare. The IC soon resigned from this implementation, too.

If an issue isn't resolved for everyone, then it isn't resolved, period. If a deliverable isn't complete for everyone, then that remains an issue until everyone is satisfied it's complete. JIP Sessions provide the forum for getting everyone concerned with an issue in one place at the same time. With JIP Sessions you can ensure that everyone participates in making the decisions and in this way you can achieve complete resolution. Figure 3.4 is an example of a list of issues jotted down by an IC.

Working the Issues

An IC *works the issues* by soliciting people's input, and by gathering relevant data and valid documentation. It takes time to understand what issues are revolving around an implementation, not getting

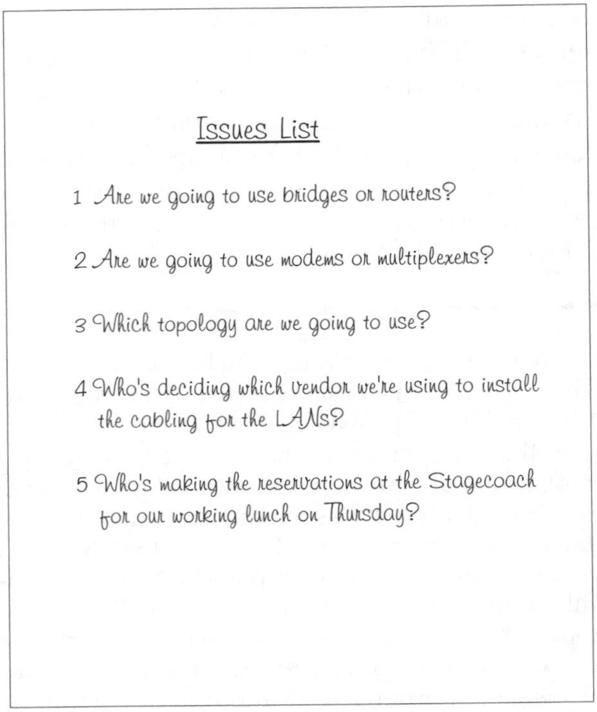

Issues List

1 Are we going to use bridges or routers?

2 Are we going to use modems or multiplexers?

3 Which topology are we going to use?

4 Who's deciding which vendor we're using to install
   the cabling for the LANs?

5 Who's making the reservations at the Stagecoach
   for our working lunch on Thursday?

Figure 3.4.   Issues List

resolved due to misunderstandings amongst the various groups. When an implementation gets hung up, it's usually because of *open issues*. By identifying and clarifying the open issues, misunderstandings can get resolved and the implementation can go forward to the next stage. To promote understanding and ultimately cooperation, the IC acts as the liaison among the various groups and tries to clear up misunderstandings. It's diplomacy in action. You hear one side's story and then you talk to the other side. You keep going back and forth, massaging the issue(s) until you can build a *bridge of agreement* between the principals.

Despite the best intentions, ICs sometimes encounter people who refuse to be reasonable or cooperative in the JIP Session when an attempt is being made to resolve an issue. The IC must then seek leverage on these people to force them to cooperate or at least to stop them from putting up resistance. Leverage can be discreet (like getting their senior manager to point the way) or blatant (like strong-arming them with threats of not supporting their implementation). It's best to use these tactics only when all else has failed and your implementation date is in jeopardy. However, it's the IC's responsibility to work every open issue to its resolution and ensure that the implementation goes forward.

Work Arounds

"Work arounds" are when you side step the organization's policies and/or procedures to resolve a problem. When people speak of "work arounds" what they're really saying is they want to put off dealing with an issue in the hope that it won't become a problem. Obviously, ICs would like to resolve every possible issue before the implementation's due date. Therefore, ICs have problems with organizations that condone "work arounds" as an acceptable mode of implementation. ICs pull their hair out on these implementations when someone acknowledges an issue has risk but would rather see if it becomes a problem than seek to resolve it right away. Typically, they will state, "If it becomes a problem we'll work around it." Merely acknowledging an issue is neither a solution nor a resolution. It is paramount that issues be resolved in order to ensure an implementation's success.

Once upon an implementation, the programmers discovered a glitch in the application code during integration testing. However, the programmers were never able to consistently duplicate the problem or determine its cause in the source code. The problem was not trivial. Every debit was being turned into a credit. The IC wanted to implement a "fix" for the problem but the Project Manager said, "It rarely seems to happen in test and has never occurred in the production environment. I don't see the point in fixing something that might never happen. If it does become a problem in production we'll just work around it at that time." One night it did become a problem as 25 million dollars worth of debits were being posted as credits! The IC, the Project Manager, and every one else high and low in the organization was at the data center at 3 A.M. trying to figure out how to fix the problem and also recover from the disaster it had caused. It was an all-time debit fiasco. Careers were jeopardized and the organization was put at risk. This would not have happened if the Project Manager had listened to the IC and not relied on the infamous "work around" as the modus operandi.

Who Is Going to Do the Work?

In every implementation someone or some group is going to have to do more work than others. That's just the way it is. Distributing the workload is one of the IC's toughest jobs. Therefore, the IC needs to state a Rule of Thumb to show everyone involved that the distribution of the workload isn't capricious or arbitrary.

> *Rule of Thumb: The person(s) or group(s) that must expend the least amount of effort to achieve the required result will do the work.*

Once upon an implementation, the people in one application group said they would get the data they needed from a file produced by an upstream application group. The upstream group's plan was to dump all their files to a dataset and the downstream application group could pick out what they wanted. However, the downstream group said they didn't want to write a subsystem to pick out and sort the data they needed. They wanted the upstream application group to write a program to produce a file in a prespecified format that contained only those data elements they requested. At this point the upstream application group said they hadn't planned to build a new file that contained only those data elements requested by the downstream application group. The IC was confronted with the classic stand-off. She had to negotiate and arbitrate about who was going to do the work. She utilized an IC's Rule of Thumb to resolve this problem.

It's helpful when dealing with matters of differences in workload to remind everyone of the *equality of tasks*. All tasks must be completed for the implementation to be successful. This will reinforce the Rule of Thumb during negotiations.

Assigning Tasks

When looking for someone to accept responsibility for a task, the IC first asks for volunteers. If that fails then someone must be chosen. Many organizations utilize a seniority or political clout paradigm. If you're at the bottom, you do the work. ICs utilize the Rule of Thumb already presented and have found that it works very well.

The person or group for whom the task is easiest to perform should do the work. If you present this in a JIP Session everyone can see the simplicity of the solution and will usually support it—especially if they understand that this rule will apply to everyone throughout the life of the implementation. If all else fails, then it's time to find an owner for the orphaned task. How to find an owner for an orphaned task is described in Chapter 10.

ACKNOWLEDGMENT

ICs always acknowledge worthy contributors to the implementation effort in a timely and accurate manner. They acknowledge stupid errors in the same way. They write and circulate all relevant documentation as quickly as they can after each JIP Session, knowing that people need the feedback, whether positive or negative. On one occasion, after an IC noted in the session write-up that everyone attended except one person who said she was "too busy," senior management replaced that person with someone else the very next day.

People want to be treated like individuals and respected for their individuality. People want to be given valuable work to do, and the opportunity to correct their work. They appreciate being acknowledged when they do well and being informed when they aren't doing so well. One of the worst things you can do is not inform participants of opportunities to improve their performance.

Rewards

ICs try to generate enthusiasm for the implementation and communicate to the participants that the success of the implementation is

the result of a team effort. If the implementation succeeds, everybody succeeds—and if it doesn't, everybody fails. ICs are cheerleaders as the implementation goes forward and point out verbally and with e-mail those people who are making contributions.

Parties and Perks

People also need to be acknowledged on a spontaneous or impromptu basis. If you just roll out the traditional perks at the prespecified time (e.g., coffee mugs after three months), people won't be motivated. Buttons, pens, mugs, and parties are great once the implementation is successful, but they can promote a false sense of security if they are given out too early in the process. However, it is good to spread plenty of everyday praise and sincere encouragement. Also, don't schedule the "implementation success party" until success is achieved—let it be a motivational perk to strive for.

CONCLUSION

To be an effective IC you need to deal with stress and ambiguity. Even though an implementation date is a long way off, the IC acts as if it's tomorrow, because everything must be in place by installation day. ICs treat every implementation as if it could put the organization out of business if it were to fail. Anything less would be unprofessional. ICs believe it's better to err on the side of caution, but don't let this become an excuse for missing an implementation date. If properly coordinated and facilitated, every implementation should be on time.

> *There is only enough data to cause paralysis—never enough to make the perfect decision.*
>
> *—Guy Kawasaki*

Stay Loose

Once all the implementation design is complete and you begin the implementation itself, detach yourself from all your planning and prepare to be completely flexible and relaxed. Remember, "Murphy lives!" and will play havoc with your best-laid plans and intentions. Figure 3.5 enumerates Murphy's Laws.

Things Happen

Ugly things do happen to ICs. If it happens to you, go straight to the Project Manager and say, "Here's what I did. Here's what I thought I was supposed to be doing. Here's what happened. What do you

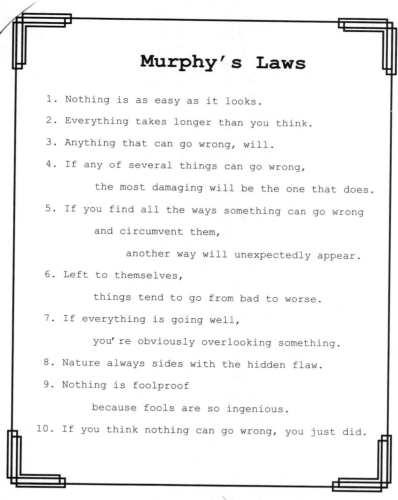

```
            Murphy's Laws

  1. Nothing is as easy as it looks.

  2. Everything takes longer than you think.

  3. Anything that can go wrong, will.

  4. If any of several things can go wrong,

          the most damaging will be the one that does.

  5. If you find all the ways something can go wrong

          and circumvent them,

              another way will unexpectedly appear.

  6. Left to themselves,

          things tend to go from bad to worse.

  7. If everything is going well,

          you're obviously overlooking something.

  8. Nature always sides with the hidden flaw.

  9. Nothing is foolproof

          because fools are so ingenious.

 10. If you think nothing can go wrong, you just did.
```

Figure 3.5.   **Murphy's Laws**

want me to do to clean it up?" Usually the Project Manager will support you. Sometimes they won't. It's all part of being an IC.

> Once upon an implementation, the IC was performing a night test on a system to be implemented which involved a number of people working statewide at many sites. The IC had set up the test so that a network of pagers coordinated everyone involved. After the test was completed, the current system was supposed to be brought up into the production environment—although it was known that every time the current system was brought up it was subject to problems, including many components that could go down statewide. When the test was completed and it was time to bring the current system back up, a ranking technical specialist said, "No problem; Operations Group can handle it from here. They've done it before." The IC was faced with a dilemma. Should she countermand this person and keep everyone on site for another two hours until 4 A.M. in case something went wrong, or trust that the Operations could get the job done? The IC didn't want to unnecessarily keep the test personnel up until the wee hours of the morning, so she took the technical specialist's word and sent everyone home. At 6 A.M. the IC got paged by the Project Manager who said, "The entire state is down. Nothing is working!" When the IC arrived at the office that day she went directly to the Project Manager and said, "Fire me; I screwed up; I should have known better." The Project Manager in this case declined the IC's offer—but this illustrates the kind of situations you will face. You don't want to countermand someone's order, but there are times when you need to follow your intuition.

Is Being an IC Worth It?

ICs find that when they've worked all night for seven nights in a row, their strength wanes and they start to get weird. In those spaces of sleep deprivation, stress, and feeling guilty about the implementation's progress, ICs experience self-doubt and question their choice of occupation. They even think about assuming positions of less responsibility just so they can be spared the IC's aggravations. Make no mistake: As an IC, you put yourself on the firing line—and you will get shot at.

On the other hand, ICs are challenged and stimulated by the

formidable tasks confronting them. They discover that new levels of difficulty only make the job more interesting. Job boredom—doing the same tasks again and again—rarely troubles an IC because there are always bigger problems to solve. ICs are always learning more about their own skills and weaknesses. This alone makes being an Implementation Coordinator worth it.

Reflect and Add Value

The ability to reflect and assess yourself and your performance is crucial to your continual improvement. ICs don't rest on their laurels. They understand that what is past is history, and that a person's reputation is made today. Therefore, reflect on your performance and try to *add value* to the implementation every day. Adding value makes every day a challenge, keeps you alert, and can actually be fun.

CHAPTER 4

Joint Implementation Process (JIP): The JIP Workshop Technique

Joint Implementation Process (JIP) is a workshop technique that is an outgrowth of implementation meetings organized and facilitated by Implementation Coordinators (ICs) in the field. The series of workshops convened over the course of an implementation are designated JIP Sessions. The JIP terminology and taxonomy of JIP Sessions are the author's invention.

Information systems are so complex that people must work together to get substantive work done. All the coordinated work of an implementation gets done in JIP Sessions. When you interact face-to-face, everyone can react immediately to objections and unpro-

ductive arguments can be squelched. In JIP Sessions you can frame the issues, define the problems, and clarify everyone's individual tasks. All the participants are able to eliminate doubts and confusion about the purpose and procedures of the implementation.

In a JIP Session a group of professionals can develop their joint skills and foster a joint body of knowledge that exceeds any individual participant's body of knowledge. To coin a phrase, the sum is greater than the parts. With most implementations, typically management wants one thing, the business users want another thing, and the technical specialists have yet something else in mind. JIP Sessions provide a forum at which everyone can sit down together and talk the issues through. These sessions constitute the IC's most important tool for generating ideas, sharing information, and making collective decisions. JIP Sessions are task oriented, collaborative, and graphic.

> *The Joint Implementation Process (JIP) is a synergy of disciplines for the knowledge-intensive information systems industry.*

There is a hidden cost to unproductive meetings. Industry studies estimate that the cost of time lost due to ineffective meetings is more than $1,000 per year per employee. You've probably observed that after an unproductive meeting, people will congregate in the hall, and bitch and moan for quite a while before they return to their desks. Conversely, when a meeting is productive, people are excited and can't wait to get back to their desks and get to work. ICs have conducted JIP Sessions at which so much was accomplished that people were "high fiving" one another at the end. People feel good when they sense they are part of an implementation that is going somewhere. A well-orchestrated JIP Session can instill those feelings and boost morale.

JIP VS. JAD

Joint Implementation Process (JIP) and Joint Application Development (JAD) are both facilitated workshops for specific purposes. JIP and JAD share similar tools (i.e., flip charts, white boards, scribes, etc.) and facilitation techniques (i.e., handling conflict, encouraging shy participants, utilizing humor, etc.). However, JIP and JAD are most dissimilar with regard to when they are utilized in the Systems Development Life Cycle (SDLC) and their purpose. JAD Sessions are conducted in the initial phase of the SDLC to define user requirements for purposes of developing an information system. JIP Sessions are conducted in the later stages of the SDLC to address the issues and problems of implementing that information system into the operational environment. JIP Sessions are an outgrowth of the JAD workshops. JIP, like every other innovation, stands on the shoulders of its forebears.

THE POWER OF COLLABORATING

The collaborative nature of JIP Sessions is conducive to joint problem solving. Many times ICs have witnessed sessions at which someone will state that there is no way an objective can be achieved—and then someone else will say, "Why don't we try this?" Sometimes, even before the issue gets written in the log, it has been resolved.

Everyone's work can be improved by input from other people. You don't lose credibility; you gain valuable insights. ICs find that people working jointly on an implementation see the value of the goal beyond themselves. They come to realize that executing the implementation in a smooth, efficient, and accurate way is of such overall value to their organization and their reputation that it transcends the importance of working on just their own piece. It isn't about individual accomplishment. It's about *joint accomplishment*, which makes *everyone* look great!

Many times, ICs witness the phenomenon of everyone believing that they were the reason for the implementation's success. It's true that the more collaboration there is on an implementation, the more important every individual feels their personal contribution to be. ICs find that JIP Sessions engender and promote the camaraderie and feedback necessary for true collaborative effort.

SERIAL INTERVIEWING

ICs figured out years ago that they shouldn't meet with people one at a time to work out implementation issues. If you interview people serially you will never resolve the contradictions. You must get everyone concerned with an issue in the same room or the only thing you will achieve is finger-pointing. The ineffectiveness of the serialized interviewing technique was the genesis of the Joint Application Design (JAD) workshop that was developed by Chuck Morris at IBM in 1977. The acronym JAD has evolved since then and is now know as Joint Application Development. The JAD workshop defines user requirements and system specifications at project inception. This front-end requirements definition is important, but there is still a long way to go to reach the final implementation of the system. By contrast, the JIP workshops resolve implementation issues on the back-end of the project.

Types of Joint Implementation Process (JIP) Sessions:

1. *Implementation Kickoff*   Convened at the start of every implementation, this session gives a broad overview of the implementation and its implications.
2. *Implementation Planning*   This session is for developing a plan of action for implementing the system or product.
3. *Business Process ReEngineering*   This session is for analyzing and modeling the organization's current work-flow.
4. *Interface Design*   This session is for defining each interface created by the system or product being implemented.
5. *Test Planning*   This session is for developing and documenting the implementation testing effort.
6. *Test-Kit Synchronization*   This session determines how to get all the test-kits to operate in unison.
7. *Test Case Development*   This session is for developing outlines for testing particular functions of the system or product to be implemented.
8. *Contingency Planning*   This session is for developing action plans for possibilities the implementation must be prepared against.
9. *Disaster Recovery*   This session is for analyzing the situation and determining how best to respond to a disaster.
10. *Problem Solving*   This session is for defining a problem, and then brainstorming and developing a solution.
11. *Customer Contact Strategy*   This session is for determining how the sales representatives are going to talk to the customers about the system or product to be implemented.
12. *Training Strategy*   This session is for developing any training required.

13. *Walk Throughs*   This session is for reviewing a group's implementation documentation.
14. *Status Sessions*   This session is for sharing information about the problems and progress of the implementation.
15. *Working Sessions*   This session is a subset of the more formalized JIP Session. It is utilized for working on an issue that impacts just a few persons or groups.
16. *Preplanning Sessions*   This session is for defining the tasks that need to get done in the formal JIP Session.

JIP SESSIONS

JIP Sessions assemble people at various stages of the implementation; with the IC's facilitation, these people cooperatively confront issues and tasks. It's an ongoing process that requires calling people together again and again. The composition of these sessions keeps changing because you only call those participants who are pertinent to the issue or task at hand. The IC always asks, "Who are the people that need to be involved to address this situation?"

JIP Sessions provide a forum for building everyone's knowledge base of the environment and applications involved in the implementation. This is crucial because many times some groups don't understand what agony the implementation is going to cause other groups. Sharing this information can promote empathy and a lot of support that wouldn't normally be forthcoming. JIP Sessions also provide the participants with an opportunity to state their business case for what they want out of the implementation. ICs find in JIP Sessions that the participants are very good at representing their own interests. You can depend on them doing that.

The Setting

The *setting* is the environment the IC creates for the JIP Session. ICs strive to create an environment in which people can deal with each other, talk about what their issues really are, be creative, and have a free-flowing exchange of ideas. What ICs want to happen is an interaction amongst peers that produces *spontaneous invention*. Interestingly enough, ICs find that what happens is invariably what needs to happen. If the right people are in attendance in the proper setting, the issues that need to be negotiated will get resolved.

The Introduction

A preliminary talk is typically given by the IC at the JIP Session. How much of an introduction is necessary is determined by how much the participants know coming in. After an IC has conducted a number of JIP Sessions for a particular implementation, the participants know who the IC is, what her role is, what the implementation's goal is, and so forth. If it's the first JIP Session and the IC is pulling people together who have never worked together before, then she initially spends a lot of time making sure everyone knows:

1. What you're trying to implement.
2. Who's playing what roles.
3. What's the company's mission.
4. What's the division's mission.
5. What's the group's mission.

However, you must always be sensitive about wasting people's time and boring them to the point of disinterest or noncooperation. Use discretion and don't over-formalize the introduction; cover what needs to be covered and then move on before people are snoring or throwing tomatoes.

Feeding the Initiative

An IC must "feed the initiative" of everyone in attendance at a JIP Session. For example, with two dozen people in the session, typically most of them won't say anything. They are intimidated by the forum, so it is up to the IC to draw them out. First, the IC recognizes each person by name and asks them to introduce themselves. There is always something special about having people introduce themselves. They can't go comatose and pretend they aren't there. If it's an especially tough group and the IC wants to soften the edges, she might say, "Tell us something interesting about yourself" or "Say something you would like everyone to know." Sometimes people will even offer something endearingly weird about themselves like, "I'm Dick Richard, and I have three cats and an intimidated dog."

Preparation

JIP Sessions require a lot of preparation. Do your homework so that you are at least on a par with everyone else's knowledge base. Don't waste the participants' time seeking information about the resident applications and the effort already expended toward the implementation. Don't fall on your face by trying to conduct sessions when you aren't already familiar with the background of the product or system to be implemented.

Have You Thought These Questions Through Before Calling a JIP Session?

Objectives	Why have a JIP Session?
Type	Which JIP Session to call?
Size	How many people in the JIP Session?
Composition	Who should attend?
Coverage	How do you make sure that everyone will be there?
When	Starting time?
Constraints	Length of the session?
Where	Is a direction map necessary?
Configuration	What is the room layout (seats, desks, etc.)?
Logistics	Is the room reserved?
Facilities	What is available (visual aids, electrical outlets, etc.)?
Agenda	Will one be published?
Presentations	Will there be any?
Documentation	What is required?

JIP Session Tools

There are five major tools that ICs utilize for JIP Sessions. These tools are described in detail in this section. These five tools are by no means the definitive list. As an IC you might invent or adapt other tools that are of particular value to you in your JIP Sessions.

JIP Session Tools
1. Task Log
2. Issues Log
3. Matrixes
4. Session Boards
5. Session Notes

Task Log.   A task is a job that needs to get done. The Task Log details who is responsible for getting those jobs done. In the JIP Sessions at which the participants break down the plan until it's obviously one person's or one group's job to do, then that person's or group's name, a description of the task, and other relevant information are written on the Task Log. So the IC would say, "Jan, you say it's your group's task to install the software on the server and it's now on the Task Log. Let us know what you need and when you'll be done." The Task Log contains all tasks relevant to the implementation whether those tasks are for an individual, a group, a division, etc. Figure 4.1 is an example of a Task Log.

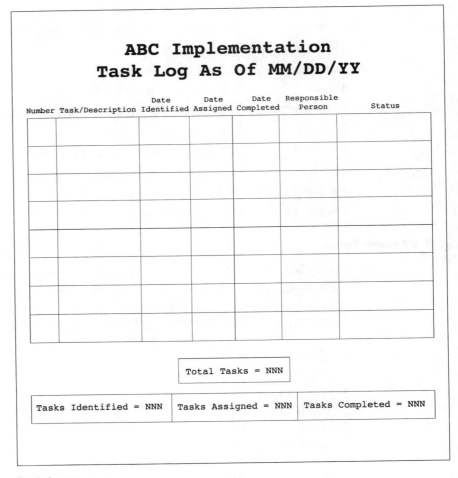

Figure 4.1.   Task Log

Issues log.   An issue is anything that is in dispute or unresolved. Many times the phrase "open issue" is used to denote a lack of resolution. When issues surface, the IC enters them into the Issues Log and makes sure it's known whose responsibility it is to get a resolution. So the IC would say, "Gene, you say you want to find out what protocol the Telecommunications Group will let us use on the organization's enterprise network. This issue is now on the Issues Log. Let us know what you find out." If it isn't evident who should be responsible for an issue, then the IC accepts ownership of that issue. The IC will then have to do some research and perhaps call another JIP Session to get the right people together to resolve the issue. Figure 4.2 is an example of an Issues Log.

When an IC says an issue is "logged," that means it has been entered into the Issues Log. It's the IC's responsibility to "work" the Issues Log. Implementations with no one to work the issues are in big trouble because the technical specialists don't have time to do it themselves. ICs try to *force the issues* by having lots of JIP Sessions early in the implementation. This gets the programmers and business users going. By articulating the issues, the JIP Session attendees can start thinking, "How can this be resolved?"

Matrixes.   ICs use matrixes all the time because we are a visual society, and these graphical charts can define and help clarify topics under discussion. ICs use matrixes so much that they even tend to make light of them by saying, "Well, here comes another matrix." The matrixes are put on the Session Boards. Figure 4.3 is an example of a responsibility matrix drawn on the Session Boards.

Session Boards.   Session Boards are large sheets of paper that are taped around the walls of the room. While the JIP Session participants are trying to crystallize an issue or concept, the designated "Scribe" writes the ideas the group produces on the Session Boards. Scribbling notes is not as effective as writing ideas on the Session Boards in front of people. By writing the issue or idea on the Session Boards and then working it, the group comes up with a good description. When everyone agrees on the description, it makes it much easier to find a solution.

The IC will always accept incomplete ideas and put them on the Session Boards because she knows people don't always think in well-formed prose. What's great about the Session Boards is the

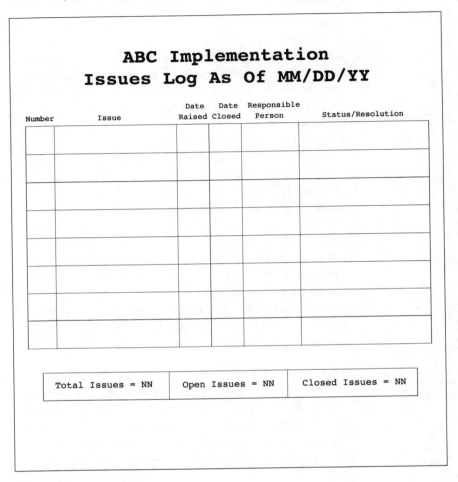

Figure 4.2.   Issues Log

way they work to improve ideas: when an ill-formed idea is "boarded" (written on the Session Boards), everyone has an opportunity to improve upon it. Ultimately you will end up with a well-discussed and sensible idea. Session Boards are also excellent devices for recognizing someone's idea. You may think someone's idea is pretty twisted, but you can acknowledge it (and more importantly, the person who suggested it) as legitimate by including the idea on the Session Boards. If the idea is really from left field, you don't have to say anything because the group will recognize that and simply pass on it.

	Work Flow	Current Implementation	New Implementation	Business Issues	Data Issues	Process Issues	Software Issues	Hardware Issues	Evaluation	Alternatives	Constraints	Risks	Plan
David Hansen	✓		✓						✓			✓	
Patty Bell					✓		✓						
Ralph Meyers				✓							✓		
Susan Tsui						✓	✓						
George Birdsong		✓							✓				
Rodrigo Santos											✓		✓
Don Von Rotz	✓		✓							✓	✓		
Joan Quick					✓		✓				✓		
Julie Marsh		✓					✓						
Victor Chan			✓	✓					✓				

Figure 4.3. **Session Board Matrix**

It would be a good idea to utilize Session Boards in every JIP Session. However, it isn't always possible or practical. Whether you use them or not should depend on the disparity of knowledge among the JIP Session participants. When the knowledge gaps are large, there is a big advantage in having all the information on the Session Boards for everyone to see. If the group participants are equally knowledgeable, you may choose not to use Session Boards.

Because you can make copies of it, you can be more expansive when you use a white board. Being able to make copies of the board for everybody means that the participants can leave the JIP Session with the product of the discussion in their hands.

In his book, *Shared Minds: The New Technologies of Collaboration*, Michael Schrage speaks about using new technologies for conducting meetings. One particular technology that Schrage discusses—having laptops in the room with the screen being projected onto the wall—sounds very suitable to JIP Sessions. If that was done everything could be recorded and saved without big sheets of butcher paper. However, most ICs continue to use White Boards or butcher paper, not yet having been afforded this type of technology.

Session Notes.   The Session Notes consist of the four tools noted here:

1. Task Log
2. Issues Log
3. Matrixes
4. Session Boards

The combination of these tools documents the core of what happens in the JIP Session. However, you can't publish these tools in their raw form. They must be reworked. The IC is responsible for reworking the tools and publishing the Session Notes. ICs try to have the tools comprise about 90 percent of the Session Notes. It isn't a good idea to surprise anyone by adding something you thought of later. If an issue got resolved between the time the JIP Session was held and the Session Notes were published then you should state that. "This didn't happen in the JIP Session but here is what I found out." Be sure you're consistent with what was said in the JIP Session because you want the Session Notes to reflect what everybody saw happen. Obviously some verbiage is required to flesh out the Session Notes. You may get lucky and receive editorial help from another person who was in the room, or maybe the person will write the Session Notes and you can edit their document. Either way the Session Notes should be published and distributed as fast as possible; not only is communication the key to success, but you will gain a lot of respect for getting out the information promptly.

JIP Session Notes Include:
1. Who was there
2. Decisions reached
3. Tasks defined
4. Task responsibility
5. Issues identified
6. Issue responsibility
7. Session boards
8. Whatever else is pertinent or helpful

The Role of the Scribe

The "Scribe" is the person designated to transcribe the group's ideas, decisions, and matrixes on the Session Boards. If the IC doesn't use Session Boards, then the Scribe just takes notes in the JIP Session. In some JIP Sessions the group may be so small that the IC can also assume the role of the Scribe. In these situations the IC ends up scribbling like a maniac while facilitating as well. It's clear that you can be more effective when you designate a Scribe to assist you in the JIP Session. For a full-blown JIP Session, you absolutely must have a Scribe in order to keep track of everything going on.

Be very careful whom you designate as your Scribe. Someone can be terrifically informed about the implementation, know all about information systems, may in fact be the business user, and a bright person—and yet produce notes that are awful. The biggest problem tends to be omission of information rather than commission of errors. If they fail to record something into the Session Notes, it's likely lost forever. You can end up very disappointed when you discover missing content in the Session Notes.

Make the effort to identify who might be a good Scribe, and then try to coerce or cajole that person (by buying lunch, for example) into being the Scribe for upcoming JIP Sessions. Not everyone makes a good Scribe. If the person understands too little of what is being said they will be very slow. They will constantly *interrupt the flow of the discussion* to get the nomenclature and acronyms right. You will be sabotaging your own JIP Session if you choose someone as the Scribe who doesn't understand the terminology of the information systems industry and so cannot go with the flow of the conversation. Critical JIP Sessions with a lot of heavy-duty technicians in attendance have been destroyed by the use of a Scribe who was not familiar with the technical jargon. Don't be hindered by someone who asks such questions as, "How do you spell CICS?" You don't want to waste the time of your high-priced talent because you have to educate your Scribe along the way.

There are usually some capable people in every JIP Session who could be the Scribe and still play their own roles. Playing two roles doesn't have to be mutually exclusive. ICs have had good success employing regular JIP Session participants as Scribes. Sometimes people even volunteer to serve as the Scribe for the next JIP Session, especially after reading the inadequate Session Notes from the previous JIP Session.

Naming the JIP Sessions

ICs usually come up with names for JIP Sessions such as: JIP Implementation Planning, JIP Interface Design, JIP Contingency Planning, and so forth. These names are useful during an implementation to help the participants understand the function of that particular JIP Session. However, there are many times when an IC working on an implementation will just use the term "Working Session." When the participants know what is going to be discussed in a particular JIP Session—because of e-mail received and previous JIP Sessions attended—then a descriptive title isn't absolutely necessary.

JIP Working Sessions

JIP Working Sessions are subsets of a more formalized JIP Session. Working Sessions are called continually by the IC over the course of an implementation. For example, suppose it's evident that an issue involves just three systems groups out of the twelve in attendance at a JIP Session. The IC might say, "OK, we've got that issue logged, now we need to work out a time when you three groups can get together and work the issue through." These situations happen all the time. You don't have to be a psychic to figure out when to call a Working Session. The people in the JIP Session will tell you, "We need to get together to discuss this issue." All you have to do is assess what's going on in the room. If people are yawning over here and looking at their watches over there, it's evident this issue doesn't affect everyone. It's then time to log the issue in the Issues Log and put together a Working Session of just those groups affected.

JIP Preplanning Sessions

ICs usually hold a JIP Preplanning Session before any major JIP Session (for example, JIP Implementation Planning, JIP Interface Design, JIP Test Planning, and so forth). At these Preplanning Sessions the IC will make a list of tasks that need to get done in the JIP Session being planned. The IC invites and expects every group that will be in the JIP Session to be represented in the Preplanning Session. The Preplanning Sessions can take from one to two hours. One task that comes out of every Preplanning Session is exactly what people need to confer about, an issue relative to that JIP Session (which could be about their area of expertise or their application's design, or their group's protocol for data exchange, and so forth). By letting people know in the Preplanning Session that they will have to do a presentation, you cause them to start thinking ahead of time about what the issues are. After all, when you know you have to make a presentation, you start thinking about what you're going to say. ICs know that the prospect of making a presentation really debugs the presenter's thinking on that subject.

It is important to state what you expect from people at the Preplanning Session. One request ICs always make is for everyone to read the background material (such as project charter, feasibility study, and so forth). When people come to a JIP Session and they have made no attempt to read the background material, they ask a lot of time-consuming questions that everyone who has read the material knows the answers to already. ICs are not above saying, "Maybe you should read the background material." The inference of such a statement is that that person should get with the program.

All-Day JIP Sessions

After the IC makes sure that everyone is in the right JIP Session, she should announce when lunch and breaks will be taken, where the phones and bathrooms are located, and any other logistical information that is pertinent. When it's a JIP Session critical to the implementation, you should establish some rules of etiquette. Ask everyone to silence their pagers or at least put them on vibrate-only mode.

ICs keep the pace of every JIP Session ongoing and lively. Energy levels are crucial to the success of JIP Sessions. When the energy in the group begins to dissipate noticeably, it's better to end the JIP Session and pick it up another day. It's like the old adage, "Leave the party while it's still going."

As a rule, all-day JIP Sessions are not a good idea. It's difficult for anyone to sit for an entire day discussing any subject, and with technical material it's beyond the call of duty. Your mind starts to wander and you just can't hold your attention to the matter at hand. ICs usually prefer half-day JIP Sessions. With half-day sessions the participants have the afternoon to mull over what was discussed in the morning, and can then show up the next day with fresh perspectives and insightful questions. However, half-day JIP Sessions may be a luxury you can't afford. Many times the pressure of an impending implementation date is such that you just don't have any choice but to hold all-day JIP Sessions.

Multiple-Day JIP Sessions

JIP Sessions requiring multiple days don't have to run on consecutive days. ICs have had success with scheduling off-days as part of multiple-day JIP Sessions. Off-days give everyone the opportunity to assimilate the information received during the previous day(s) and to structure it in terms of the "big picture." The IC should assemble and bind the Session Notes from the previous day's session into a convenient and usable format. Then the next day of the JIP Session, you can say, "Here's what we covered in the JIP Session so far. We dealt with these topics . . . , we got this far . . . , we saw that this group needs . . . ," and so forth.

Sometimes it's impossible to do all the work required for a particular stage of an implementation even in a multiple-day JIP Session. Time constraints are a fact of life in business. While you may not be able to amplify specifications down to the level of detail necessary for making changes, you can identify the issues that must be addressed and then prioritize that list. Most importantly, form a task force that will work on these issues, and then make sure there is agreement on when its work will be done and what its deliverables should look like. The JIP Session participants should all approve whoever volunteers or is chosen to represent them on the task force. This process of forming a task force, designating a due date, and defining deliverable(s), will spawn the next JIP Session.

Electronic JIP Sessions

Sometimes implementations involve working with participants at remote sites. This is when the "electronic" technologies of video teleconferencing, conference phone calling, and electronic forums come into play. These technologies save a lot of money on travel expenses and enable the IC to facilitate JIP Sessions for national and international organizations. Video teleconferencing uses a video camera at each site so the JIP Session participants can see as well as hear one another. Conference phone calling uses a speakerphone at each site so the JIP Session participants can at least speak with one another. Both these technologies have been used quite successfully for JIP Sessions involving many people at far-flung locations.

Forums are software packages or online networking services that facilitate interactive meetings through everyone's PC. Forums are starting to find application in the organizational world. The concept of interactively conversing with others through a computer appeals to many people. However, although forums can be useful, we're still a long way from digitizing our reality and transcending the need for face-to-face or at least ear-to-ear interaction. So forums aren't really practical for JIP Sessions. However, forums can be valuable for generating a discussion on a specific question or idea, such as: "Has anyone implemented a local-area network on multiple platforms with dissimilar operating systems and protocols?" Since the forum can be broadcast and accessed organization-wide, it's an opportunity to tap a very broad body of knowledge. What makes forums different from e-mail messaging is that any user can follow another user's response. It's an organization-wide interactive discussion (forum) that anyone can listen to, and join in if desired.

Publishing an Agenda

What you will find is that people want an agenda published before the JIP Session so they know what topics are being discussed in which order. However, some people want this information only because they don't want to attend the JIP Session except when their application or area of responsibility is being discussed. Agendas can quickly degenerate into laundry lists that can be checked for the inclusion of the dirtiest items. Therefore, especially for JIP Sessions critical to the implementation, the IC may choose not to publish or even refuse to publish an agenda for some JIP Sessions. Why would you want everyone to attend for the entire JIP Session? Because it's important for the *joint process* that all JIP Session participants be present. It's difficult to predict in which order issues will be discussed and how much time each issue may consume. Going into the JIP Session, you usually don't even know what all the issues are. You're holding the JIP Session to identify, define, and if possible, resolve the issues. To do that you need the participants to work interactively. This isn't going to happen if the holders of key information are not present in the JIP Session when those issues are discussed. When you go ahead without a prepublished agenda, remember that the participants are entering a seemingly unstructured JIP Session, so your introductory talk that details the JIP Session's purpose, goals, and other pertinent information is especially important.

Straw Documents

A "straw document" is a prototype of the document the JIP Session participants need to produce in a particular JIP Session. The IC brings the straw document to the JIP Session but she isn't attached to it and doesn't care if it's refuted. The reason for a straw document is that it can expedite the JIP Session by providing a prototype from which the JIP Session participants can work. ICs use straw documents for developing different types of plans for the implementation. The IC can walk into the JIP Session and say, "Here's a straw plan I made up that outlines some of the tasks we need to accomplish in order to get this system implemented. What did I leave out?

What's in the wrong order? What needs to be expanded or clarified?" Straw documents make it easier for people by providing them with an outline to modify or build upon.

Once upon an implementation, the IC was having trouble getting a particular group to commit to attending a JIP Interface Design Session because its people didn't understand that the JIP Interface Specification Document (ISD) they had already produced wasn't adequate. So the IC provided this group with a straw document of the JIP ISD Document she wanted them to produce once all the issues were resolved in the JIP Session. When the attendees understood what the IC was trying to achieve in the session and saw that the process had an end, they willingly committed to participating in the JIP Interface Design Session.

ADMINISTERING JIP SESSIONS

The IC should administer the JIP Sessions so that the IC can manage the session's structure and direction. However, ICs never seek to control the content of the JIP Session; they only want to provide the forum in which the participants can visualize how they will achieve their goal(s). Then it's up to the participants to decide what tasks must get done. In addition, they can identify the possible pitfalls and risks, and determine themselves how those factors will be addressed.

Once upon an implementation, the IC was in a meeting at which she felt manipulated by the senior manager. She came to the meeting believing it was to be a brainstorming session. But she gradually realized that what was really happening was a prearranged scenario in which the attendees were just eliminating every option until they got down to the senior manager's idea. The IC was offended by the fact that neither she nor anyone else in attendance was really in the meeting for any other reason than to endorse the senior manager's idea. In their own JIP Sessions, ICs strive very hard not to let this happen; JIP Session participants should never feel manipulated or coerced.

Starting up the Session

The IC starts the initial JIP Session with an introductory talk and then concludes by asking, "What is the purpose of our being together? What do we want to accomplish?" These questions will set up and spawn a discussion of the implementation's mission. Following the IC's lead, the JIP Session participants can then define, by their criteria, what constitutes "success." It's also usually worthwhile to take the time to discuss everyone's assumptions.

For subsequent JIP Sessions the IC typically gives a brief introduction and setup. The IC states what the implementation's mission is, outlines the objective(s) for that day's JIP Session, and details what the participants are trying to accomplish. She then asks, "Are we all in agreement?" By repeatedly putting the case to the participants, they come to understand that it's their JIP Session.

Standing vs. Sitting

For JIP Sessions with many participants, the IC usually addresses the group while standing. This posture of the IC gives the JIP Session a degree of formality that is usually important. For smaller JIP Sessions, the IC sits at the head of the table because that's the power position. However, if the IC is involved in a JIP Session in which she's trying to build a coalition or consensus on an issue, then she should consciously sit down and take a seat at the side of the table.

Peer-to-Peer

The IC sets the tone for the JIP Sessions by treating everyone as a professional and conducting every interaction on a *peer-to-peer* basis. The participants generally take the cue and likewise demonstrate respect towards one another. ICs who successfully set this tone experience few problems with JIP Session participants sniping at one another. Every IC certainly has situations in which the people at the JIP Session become angry or at odds with one another. After all, people are more easily upset when they don't know everybody and don't understand all the issues. In seeking to do their best, and sensing someone is in their way, they don't look at that person's side of the issue; they just want them out of their way. The IC can help such antagonists understand both sides of the issue, and come to amicable terms. Most of the time, it's just a matter of mediating as a fair witness, saying something like, "This is what they say they need, and here is what you say you need. Now how can we work something out?"

ICs feel it is "bad form" for a participant to criticize someone who isn't at the JIP Session. (At least if they rip someone who is in attendance, that person has a chance to defend herself.) However, ICs shouldn't try to be morally didactive by making a "behavior policy" statement to the group. What ICs have found to be effective is to embody the attitude and demonstrate the demeanor they expect from the JIP Session participants. Professionals working with professionals on an equal basis (peer-to-peer) is the desired mode of interaction, with no one (including the IC) taking a higher position. So if someone does make a disparaging comment during a JIP Session, the IC should say something like, "Yo gang, there's an old saying that both praise and criticism are frauds, so let's get back on track." Another technique ICs use is to exploit the disparaging comment. If someone says, "We don't want this to go bad like Fred's implementation," the IC will say, "OK, what went wrong with Fred's implementation? What can we do to make sure that this implementation doesn't have those same problems?" By appropriately exemplifying peer-to-peer interaction, you should be able to consistently maintain the focus of your JIP Sessions.

Resetting and Distilling the Issue

There are times when the IC just needs to "reset the issue," thus clarifying any misunderstandings and ensuring that everyone is "on the same page." For example, the IC says, "Remember, this is the Sales, Order, Billing (SOB) Implementation, which is about electronically capturing orders from our customers so we can invoice them and ship the goods all on the same day. The goal of our JIP Session today is to resolve the issue of reversing an invoiced account when what was delivered wasn't what the customer wanted."

At other times the IC has to "distill the issue" down to it's essence. The IC listens to many conversations and then says, "What I think we're talking about is the issue of what do we do when . . ."

Defining Roles

In JIP Sessions, everyone's role is sufficiently defined for normal purposes by having them introduce themselves with their job title. However, in some organizations more clarification may be needed because their roles are so ill-defined that no one is clear about their responsibilities. In organizations such as these, job titles mean little, and the IC has to spend a lot of time determining who should be doing what. Of course, once the role is defined that person may insist that the responsibility is someone else's. It's a common occurrence for someone to define their own role as very small while everyone else assumes that person's role is very large. This leaves the IC with major gaps in the responsibility matrix. So be aware that defining roles can be a problem, especially because it's a reflection of the organization's culture. The determining factor in everyone's role on an implementation is whether individuals are empowered by their organization to perform their particular jobs.

In some organizations, every professional employee has both a title and the responsibility that goes with it. They have the job, their name is on it, they get to do it, and they get to make the decisions. If it's beyond their responsibility to make a particular decision, they know that and can lobby with the person who is empowered to make that decision.

In other organizations, employee roles are deliberately fuzzy. People can get their decisions overridden despite their job titles. The result is that everyone feels they have very little power. These people are therefore reluctant to take any initiative or make any decisions. In these kinds of organizations the IC's job is much harder because it requires much more time and energy to determine and define each implementation participant's role, and to establish a procedure for making decisions.

About Getting Involved

Robert's Rules of Order states that the chairperson is not allowed to become involved with the content of a meeting. ICs do not adhere to this principle. Although ICs facilitate every JIP Session as the servant of the group, they still get involved with the session's content. ICs believe it's best to be constructively biased. They are usually information systems professionals with a lot of expertise gleaned from years in the field. They feel that their expertise and knowledge should be shared for the benefit of the implementation. So ICs get involved and sometimes even play the role of "devil's advocate" in an effort to create a balance within the group. Over the course of a JIP Session, the IC may take all sides at different times: the neutral observer's role, the expert's role, and the advocate's role. However, an IC needs to be detached from her own ambitions. If it's perceived that the IC is striving to aggrandize her position within the organization, or has a political goal or hidden agenda beyond the implementation, there will be problems around the issue of improper facilitation.

Implementing Structure

When facilitating a JIP Session, the IC always faces the problem that each group within an organization has its own methodology, vocabulary, and structure. For example, the various application groups won't be ready to support the different test phases at the

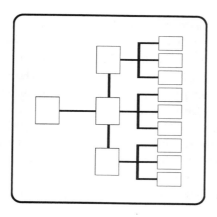

same time. When you schedule integration testing, some groups may be performing application unit testing. When you schedule user-acceptance testing, some groups may be performing integration testing within their application. The timing cycles within any cross-organizational implementation dictate that the various application groups are rarely ready for the disparate test phases at the same time. It's OK that every group has it's own methods, vocabulary, and structure. However, it's imperative that they all participate cooperatively within the implementation's structure. It's the IC's responsibility to make sure each group operates within the implementation's structure.

Institutionalizing Structure

ICs strive to bring appropriate structure to every implementation. However, an IC must constantly battle the tendency toward the institutionalization of that structure. Once a good custom or practice becomes institutionalized, it sucks life away from the implementation. A typical case of institutionalization is the way that some groups use other groups' documentation. If the first application group's JIP Interface Specification Document (ISD) is well done, then every JIP ISD produced after the first mindlessly duplicates the same structure, even though it makes no sense to have some of the elements from the first document in the subsequent documents. The IC needs to remind each group to cut out the irrelevant elements from the preceding documentation, and more importantly, to *think* about what they are producing.

System Development Life Cycle

ICs facilitating JIP Sessions have found it to be a problem when the business users (or anyone else involved) are unfamiliar with the System Development Life Cycle (SDLC) for information systems. The System Development Life Cycle is summarized as: analysis, design, code, test, and implement. Virtually everyone working with information systems is familiar with the SDLC. Still, it does happen that you'll find yourself dealing with neophytes who have never even heard of it. In these situations you need to take the time to explain what the System Development Life Cycle is and how it works. It's important that everyone has the same contextual frame of reference so the JIP Sessions can be expedited in a timely manner.

Figure 4.4.   **System Development Life Cycle**

Since JIP Sessions are about implementing information systems, all the participants need a familiarity with the phases involved. Figure 4.4 symbolically represents the five phases of the System Development Life Cycle.

BUILDING CONSENSUS

ICs have learned that the best way to resolve issues or problems is by achieving consensus. What is consensus? Consensus means that everyone is in agreement with the decision. They don't necessarily have to like the decision, but they have acceded to its implementation. The JIP Sessions provide a process for consistently reaching consensus because the participants *collaboratively* frame the problem, brainstorm for solutions, and evaluate the alternatives.

To effectively build consensus, the IC must protect the JIP Session participants. Given human nature, people will work themselves into a corner they can never get out of if they're pushed too hard. The IC needs to be sensitive enough to know when to back off (and back the group off, if necessary), so that someone can "save face." If you don't facilitate an easy way for a person to get off their bad idea, then they will have to defend it to the end. Defending their idea to the end isn't good for that person, the other participants, or the implementation. In these situations you can return to any earlier phase of the discussion as a way to ease the pressure off that person. You can say, "Let's look at how we framed that issue on the Session Boards."

If an IC senses there is a clear stand-off between two groups or two ideas, then that JIP Session probably isn't the time or place to solve it. The IC can say, "Folks, let's do some more research and pick another time that we can talk about this issue." The key is to give people some space; in the interim, some way of resolving the issue will usually arise. It also gives you an opportunity to do background work. You can wander around and talk to everyone, discovering what else can be done. Also, you can poll people about the different alternatives: "Are you sure this is the only solution you can support? Your co-worker thinks this other solution might work, so what do you think about that one?"

ICs want everyone leaving a JIP Session to have a good feeling about the decision(s) reached. With compromises, each side must make concessions—sometimes to their own system's detriment—just to reach an agreement. ICs have found that compromises tend to be half-baked solutions that don't really address the group's requirements. So you should always strive for solutions that are for the betterment of the system or product to be implemented, not just to ease the conflict or antagonism amongst the JIP Session participants.

When people agree about what they have to do, they will do a more thorough job. When you facilitate a JIP Session in which consensus has been reached, then everyone's satisfaction with the results translates into a willingness to expedite the implementation process.

Direct Consensus

ICs see no point in spending a lot of time evaluating an issue when a clearly good idea has been suggested, that is, one that everyone could possibly live with. So sometimes the IC should bypass the usual problem-solving steps and shoot directly for consensus by asking, "Is there anyone who cannot accept this solution?" JIP Sessions aren't about finding the perfect solution; they're about finding solutions that everyone can live with.

Soliciting Criticism

It's important to keep soliciting criticism from the JIP Session participants, because this works well for building consensus. After a discussion you can say, "OK, here's what I think we said. Does this make sense? Is there anything missing?" It's important to force people to get involved because there is always someone who's thinking, "I wouldn't have stated it that way." You should make sure all the participants know that they will have every opportunity to change any and every word on the Session Boards. If they don't choose to change it, then it's a "done deal" because they have given their tacit agreement. And the IC is politically protected because she can then say, "They were in that JIP Session and they agreed."

ICs are responsible for finding out everything that could possibly make an implementation fail. So you shouldn't let anyone who's involved think they're bystanders or believe they're not participating in the JIP Session. You don't want them saying, "Oh, it was those other people who let us down," because everyone is part of that process. Therefore, reiterate to the JIP Session participants that they take every opportunity to challenge anything. Try to create these opportunities by always asking, "What isn't going to work?" or "What are you worried about?" Remind them that even tomorrow, while they're brushing their teeth or driving down the highway, if they think of something that might be detrimental to the implementation, to please call and let you know!

PROBLEM SOLVING

JIP Problem Solving Sessions are essential for problem resolution. ICs will hold JIP Problem Solving Sessions until they know what the problem is and can state that problem clearly. Stating the problem with clarity takes you halfway to the solution, for without a complete description you don't understand the problem.

ICs find problem solving to be fun; it's awesome what minds working together can accomplish. Groups can more readily identify problems and generate solutions than an individual ever could. In order to focus on the essence of a problem, the IC has the Scribe keep writing and rewriting the description of the problem on the Session Boards until all the JIP Session participants agree with the description.

There are tremendous differences among describing, brainstorming, evaluating, negotiating, voting, and executive decision making. When the JIP Session participants finish with one mode and move on to the next or even go back to a previous mode, the group must shift gears. This shift needs to be explicitly and consciously recognized. Therefore, the IC points out these changes in modes to the group, and thus helps everyone come up to speed after shifting gears.

Many times in JIP Problem Solving Sessions, ICs witness someone trying to answer for or solve someone else's problem. This is especially true if the person whose application is being addressed is shy or timid. When this happens, you should restrain the person providing the answer by pointing out, "That's Craig's responsibility. So let's ask Craig." (Assuming that Craig is there in the JIP Session.) ICs want to talk to people only about what they are responsible for, and keep silent about what they are not responsible for. To deal with problems, you must talk to the person(s) responsible for them; otherwise you're wasting everyone's time.

ICs sometimes find that when a group is trying to frame a problem, the dialogue can become too abstract. It's good for everyone's understanding of the problem to move from the concrete to the abstract during the discussion. However, when the group gets hung up on generalities, the IC always grounds the conversation by asking for specifics, such as, "What do you mean response time won't be adequate?"

When facilitating a particularly difficult JIP Problem Solving Session, you want to try to keep the confidence level high, so it's a good idea to periodically point out how much the participants have accomplished so far.

Analysis and Synthesis

Analysis is the process of breaking a problem apart. Synthesis is the process of reforming those parts back into the original problem statement. This process of separation and combination is a technique that enables the JIP Session participants to thoroughly understand a problem and make sure they have the best possible solution.

> *Analysis separates a problem into its constituents while synthesis combines those constituents to form a coherent whole.*
>
> *—Ken Orr*

Whenever a group of people are assembled in a JIP Problem Solving Session, different issues and concerns are the norm, not the exception. These differences are helpful because they provide the basis for a broad spectrum of analysis and synthesis. The broader the group's perspective, the more likely it is that it will arrive at a comprehensive solution.

Dealing with Complexity

In JIP Problem Solving Sessions the information systems problems being addressed are typically very complex. For this reason, ICs utilize white boards or flip charts to diagram what the group is discussing. The Session Boards are utilized for getting agreement on the Scribe's summation of the discussions. The IC documents what is being discussed by "capturing it" on the white boards or flip charts. ICs find diagrams and matrixes can really help everyone understand what is being discussed.

In the information technology environment, the systems are usually intricate and always interconnected. Simple solutions to problems are hardly ever found. Since every application is part of a larger system, you must have a systemic (affecting the whole body)

> The purpose of dialogue is to reveal the incoherence in our thought.
>
> —David Bohm

view of the business's entire systems environment to understand how changes in one application will impact another.

Many JIP Problem Solving Sessions begin by analyzing the problem and breaking it down into sub-problems before actually attempting to form a description of the problem. This analysis process is pursued by the JIP Session participants by means of *"talking through the problem."* Systems professionals are good at talking through an issue because they have built so many systems without benefit of design models. "Talking through" used to be (and in many organizations still is) the only mechanism available to systems professionals for understanding and segmenting tasks. After talking it through, the sub-problems usually fall out, the task segmentation is evident, and what needs to be addressed in which order can be worked out.

When a number of people get together in a JIP Session to solve a problem or problems, you know that there are as many agendas coming into the room as there are people. So you can say, "We know we have to solve these problems. Does anyone else have any other problems that we should add as items to our agenda?" By taking the time at the beginning for the master agenda to be modified, the participants get the sense that they own the JIP Problem Solving Session and will assume responsibility for what happens. You can then set up the topics for discussion by stating that this particular set of people is getting together to solve this particular set of problems.

Problem Solving
1. Describing the Problem
2. Brainstorming
3. Evaluation
4. Negotiating
5. Voting
6. Executive Decision Making

Describing the Problem

When problem solving, you must first describe the problem. This means setting boundaries around it by defining what is within the topic of discussion and what is outside of it. In a JIP Problem Solving Session, when a group addresses a problem you need to remind the group that what it's trying to do is *describe the problem*. If the group cannot at least do this, they will never agree on a solution. Describing the problem establishes the range of acceptable options. Make sure the group describes the problem and does not offer solutions. "Adding more CPU capacity will increase throughput" does not describe a problem, but instead offers a solution to a still-undescribed problem. When generating a description, it helps to have everyone state their personal view of the problem.

Build a Problem-Description by Asking:
1. Whose problem is it?
2. What is the nature of the problem?
3. When is the solution deadline?

If, in trying to describe a problem, you discover that the problem impacts other groups or systems, there is little point in continuing until those other parties are invited to the JIP Problem Solving Session. You don't know *what you don't know* until these other parties are represented. Therefore, you should table this problem until the JIP Session can reconvene with everyone included. ICs make sure the right people are talking together before trying to solve any problem.

ICs have noticed a common pitfall when facilitating JIP Problem Solving Sessions. People who haven't attended any of the implementation's previous JIP Sessions but are in the JIP Problem Solving Session because they are being impacted by the problem don't know all the history and language of the implementation to date. The people who have more seniority with the problem tend to assume a level of shared understanding that may not exist. This situation can be misleading because it may sound as if people are communicating when in fact they aren't. The IC has to make sure that enough background information is presented so that everyone is "on the same page."

Once the group has described the problem and written a description with which everyone is satisfied, the most difficult part of the problem-solving process is done. After developing a written description, you now move on to determining who has to work with whom to devise a solution. Once this determination has been made the responsible person or persons and other pertinent information is noted in the Task Log.

Brainstorming

Brainstorming is how the JIP Problem Solving Session participants try to generate solutions to a problem. In the brainstorming portion of a JIP Problem Solving Session, the IC lets all those present know they can contribute. Everyone from secretaries to vice-presidents can participate in the process. Note that brainstorming for solutions is quite different from evaluating those solutions. When brainstorming, the group spontaneously voices ideas and proposals without trying to evaluate their worth. The IC needs to remind everyone not to make evaluations as they brainstorm. The only goal is to transcribe as many proposals as possible onto the Session Boards in the allotted time. Each one of the proposals will be evaluated later. When someone says "Let's test every account," and someone else says, "We can't test every account. We don't have time!" you need to say, "That's evaluation, so let's hold that for later. The idea itself is valid so it goes on the Session Boards."

When brainstorming, avoid assumptions. Always insist on hard data. When someone says, "They have never installed a change request that quickly," you can ask, "How quickly can we get a change request installed and on what historical data is that estimate based?" Also, be wary of the "experts" when they offer opinions about something outside the area of their expertise. "Experts" typically have an opinion or answer to every question, and to blindly follow their advice can have negative consequences for an implementation. (Interestingly enough, human experts tend to respond just like Expert Systems in computer software. If you ask a Medical Expert System how to fix a flat tire, it will prescribe a drug.) You can circumvent false experts by asking the participants for appropriate help: "Folks, what we need here is a bona fide expert in this particular area. Can anyone recommend who that would be? And is she here now?" If need be, invite the recommended expert(s) to the next JIP Problem Solving Session.

Evaluating

Evaluating is the process by which the JIP Problem Solving Session participants collectively agree on the merit of each proposal. Criteria may have to be established to determine which proposal among several similar proposals is the most appropriate solution for the problem being discussed. You may find it helpful to draw a matrix on the Session Boards with proposals on one axis and the criteria on the other axis, so the group will have a visual standard on which to base their opinions. Figure 4.5 is an example of a proposals/criteria matrix drawn on the Session Boards. Evaluating is more difficult than brainstorming and may involve negotiating or even Executive Decision making. Executive Decision making is explained later in this chapter.

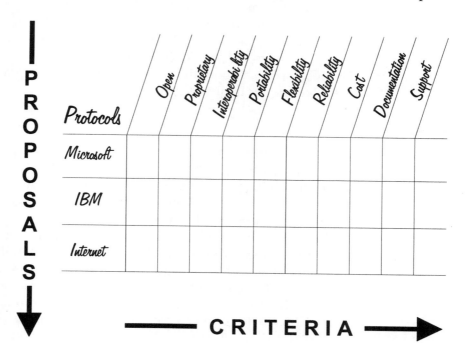

Negotiating

When evaluating proposals to solve a problem, the criteria aren't always discrete (black or white). Typically, there are things that each person and/or group participating in the JIP Session is willing to give and other things they expect to receive. So negotiating is an important component of evaluation because it really helps to get the problem-solving processes rolling forward. For example, a group can promise to include some new feature in the current release if other features (promised for the current release) are deferred until future releases.

> The more you study _convergent_ problems, the more the answers converge. The more you study _divergent_ problems, the more the answers contradict one another.
>
> —E.F. Schumacher

The problems confronted by an information systems implementation are typically _divergent problems_. Divergent problems do not have one correct solution, but rather a number of solutions of varying cost and impact. So the IC needs to keep reminding the JIP Session participants of the "divergent dilemma" they're confronting. The IC employs negotiation skills to help the group arrive at a viable solution for their divergent problem(s).

Voting

ICs try to avoid voting on potential or proposed solutions to a problem because voting frames the issue in extremes. ICs want the JIP Problem Solving Session participants to be creative in their pursuit of alternatives, not settle for simplistic either/or outcomes that may actually be conceptual deadends.

Voting in a JIP Problem Solving Session can have a negative impact on the session participants. Voting forces people to make a statement or take a stand on an issue. This tends to promote factions or heighten the sense of alienation among the implementation participants. ICs find it best not to vote but to seek mutual consent instead. Those who don't agree with the decision can then accede without creating dissension in the implementation effort. Also, when the participants vote, it implies that the decision must be made today. ICs find this isn't always the case. See if you can table the problem and look at it in another JIP Session, or at least buy some time to resolve the problem in some other way.

Executive Decision Making

One way to resolve a problem is by *Executive Decision*. In every implementation effort, the business user must specify what the system or product to be implemented is ultimately supposed to do. The business user is the "executive" who makes decisions based on the alternatives suggested by the participants of the JIP Problem Solving Session. (If there isn't anyone to make an executive decision, then the implementation is in real trouble.) When a problem is resolved by Executive Decision, it doesn't mean the JIP Session participants have wasted their time. The very process of generating alternative solutions to a problem promotes a good understanding of the complex issues that must be addressed during the implementation by the JIP Session participants. Also, the IC gains the support of those who participated in the JIP Session because those participants developed the alternatives leading up to the Executive Decision.

Once upon an implementation, the IC was facilitating a JIP Problem Solving Session in which the discussion degenerated into an argument among the technical specialists about the possible alternatives. At this point the IC said, "Let's stop discussing this problem because we have a business user who will give us an answer. I will explain the alternatives and the business user will choose one." Presently the group continued with their haggling, so the IC reiterated, "You're getting nowhere bickering about this problem. It's not your decision to make, but I will present your alternatives to the business user. Let's move on."

ICs find that the JIP Problem Solving Session participants generally like Executive Decisions because they don't have to convince each other about anything; they know that someone else is going to decide the issue. Executive Decisions are also popular because the bottom-line goal of any implementation is to satisfy the business user, and so it's easy to support an Executive Decision.

GETTING THE RIGHT PEOPLE IN THE JIP SESSION

Nothing is more integral to the success of any JIP Session than having *the right people* in attendance. Appropriate attendance is crucial to your success as an IC. If you know you need representation from five groups to completely cover an issue and only four groups show up, then you're in trouble. So you must do whatever it takes to make sure that you've got all the *coverage* you need. Coverage means that some *knowledgeable* person or persons will represent each group in the JIP Session.

Too often, if you aren't careful, some groups will send a "new hire" or programmer trainee to your JIP Session, which is the same as having no one from that group attend. It's not sufficient just to invite the groups to attend your JIP Session. You must be sure that some qualified person is going to attend. Follow up your invitation by verifying with the managers that they received it, and send e-mail reminders the day before the JIP Session. ICs have even been known to stop JIP Sessions and telephone people they had expected who weren't there. If you're missing representation from any group, then you're back to the "serial interview" scenario. Nothing can get resolved because anything decided in the JIP Session will have to be presented to and accepted by the non-attendees.

Although every IC has held a JIP Session with the wrong people in attendance, obviously you should try to prevent this from happening. Otherwise you will have people who clearly do not understand what the implementation is all about in the JIP Session representing some group. If this happens to you, before the next JIP Session you must go to the management of that group and say, "The person you sent to the JIP Session is unacceptable as your representative." You can then provide them with a list of people from their group who are acceptable because they understand your implementation and its issues.

Picking the Participants

Picking the participants is crucial to the success of every JIP Session. You should start by determining who does what to make the implementation happen. If eight systems have to make changes to support the implementation, then clearly they must all be represented. However, sometimes groups that have no responsibility should attend anyway because they could be impacted by the implementation. You might wonder, "Are the accounting people going to be affected by this implementation?" You don't know yet, but you better get someone from the comptroller's office to represent their issues, so they can feel it out. You may end up inviting people to a JIP Session whom you aren't sure will be impacted by the implementation. Typically these are compliance personnel or groups that may "need to know" about the implementation. After a couple of JIP Sessions they'll let you know if their area is impacted or not, and whether the JIP Sessions have any relevance for them.

It's better to err on the side of caution and invite too many people than to invite too few. ICs should not arbitrarily set some artificial limit on the number of people in their JIP Sessions. If you don't have all the intelligence in attendance at the JIP Session you can't be effective. You've got to open the JIP Session to everyone. It's the only way to make sure that every system or group has heard the same information.

Overcoming Resistance

It can be a grueling struggle to overcome resistance on the part of the principals to attend the JIP Sessions. The implementation date could be six months or maybe even a year away. Some application groups may have only a small part in the implementation, such as displaying one field on a screen. Since these application groups don't have much to do and the implementation date is months away, they don't even have anyone working on their part yet. However, it is still important for every group to attend the formative JIP

Implementation Planning Sessions that are held early in the implementation effort.

How can you be sure those people you need will attend your JIP Sessions? ICs find the most effective device is to show everyone how the JIP Sessions work to achieve pre-defined goals within a specified period of time. Your reputation for not wasting professionals' time will precede you. Once your goals are accomplished the professionals' attendance will no longer be required. If reputation and reason don't work, then you can implore, cajole, and even demand. After all your efforts, if some group fails to attend your JIP Sessions you should escalate that issue with your Project Manager and that group's management.

What Level Person Is Required from Each Group?

The level of person required from each application group or system depends on what you're trying to accomplish in the JIP Session you're coordinating. It's a refining process. At the first JIP Session it's best if the manager responsible for the system is in attendance. At subsequent JIP Sessions a technical specialist usually becomes the point of integrative responsibility for that group. However, during the course of the implementation, issues may be raised that require the manager's involvement again (for example, to resolve issues that the technician specialist shouldn't decide).

Auditors/Comptroller

It's always a good idea to involve the comptroller's office and auditors early on in the implementation. Tell them specifically what you need from them (for example, involvement in all the general ledger balancing). The auditors can be of tremendous value to an implementation because they have seen all the mistakes made by previous implementations and can help you avoid those same errors. Also, if the auditors are dissatisfied with your implementation, you will never be allowed to install the system or product.

CONCLUSION

One final note on JIP Sessions: *Everything is optional.* How far or how much or how long for each and every JIP Session is always variable. JIP is an inexact process that you should customize to your advantage, adapting it to the needs of your own implementation.

CHAPTER 5

What Is to Be Done?
Day One for the
Implementation Coordinator

You've been hired as an Implementation Coordinator (IC). So now what do you do on day one of the job? Well, it's a good idea to take your first cup of coffee, and then set out to determine at which stage is the implementation, right now.

PHASES AND STAGES

A "phase" is defined as a distinct period of development. While the phases of the System Development Life Cycle (SDLC) are well known (that is, analysis, design, code, test, implement), the phases of an implementation are much more vague. An implementation is probably more correctly characterized as having "stages." A stage is defined as an interval of time in the course of a process. The implementation process is a series of stages. Trying to define a taxonomy of implementation stages is all but impossible because every implementation and its problems are unique. Determining the stage of an implementation is a subjective "judgment call" made by the IC, following the answer to but one burning question:

> *What is the next major deliverable? This is where to begin.*

Where to Begin

By determining what is the next major deliverable, you will know where to begin. If the implementation planning has been done then the next major deliverable is the execution of that plan, and that is where you begin. If there is no Implementation Plan, then go back a step and begin by first coordinating the development of an Implementation Plan. There are innumerable possible scenarios. The key action is to figure out what's the next major deliverable, and then you'll know what needs doing from that point.

Ascertaining the status of the implementation effort is itself a process that can take several weeks. It's a matter of gathering all the pieces of a puzzle, and then putting them together until the image of the next big deliverable takes form. In the interim, the IC takes over the Issues Log and takes responsibility for all open issues and concerns. This also means becoming the chairperson at all meetings pertaining to the implementation. The IC also takes custodianship of the existing project or Implementation Plans. The plans given the IC at this point typically aren't what the implementation ultimately needs, but are valuable because they reflect the situation up to now, and tell what is in place at the moment. Any information about the implementation can be useful, regardless of how brief or even incorrect it may be.

Search and Discovery

Once you have determined the next major deliverable, you're ready to begin the process of *search and discovery*. This is one of the most creative and enjoyable parts of the IC's job. You wander around the organization conferring with people and gathering information— like a detective who solves a crime, or a reader who figures out the plot of a good novel. It's fun to touch all the bases, gather all the loose ends together, and sift the clues to figure out who's conscientious and who's malingering, who's forthright and who's disingenuous, who wants the implementation to succeed and who is too burned out to care. Invariably you will find miscommunication and mismatched expectations among the different groups. The IC is the go-between who provides the forum for discussion through JIP Sessions, facilitates the dialogue, and resolves the misunderstandings turned up by search and discovery.

Interviewing the Participants

The IC begins the search and discovery process by interviewing the person who assigned, recruited, or hired her for the IC position. The IC then interviews the key participants in the implementation. Interestingly, many times ICs find they don't even have to set up interviews. People just say to them, "Come talk to me and let me tell you what I think of this implementation."

Interview Questions to Ask

- How important is the implementation to the interviewee?
- What are the interviewee's issues?
- What are the interviewee's concerns?
- How does the interviewee perceive the importance of the implementation to the other participants?
- What is the interviewee's perception of the strengths and weaknesses of the person(s) or team(s) doing the work?
- What will be the impact if the system or product isn't implemented on schedule?
- What is the make-or-break issue determining whether the implementation will or will not work?
- What is the implementation's biggest challenge?

Obtaining this information will be particularly useful later on in the implementation so you can figure out what people are *really* saying. The interview process identifies what's on everyone's agenda and many times tips you to hidden agendas. You will learn what needs to be done and just what the issues are. You will also find out what are perceived to be the weak spots in the implementation effort. For example, let's say one group believes another group to be technologically weak. They will always blame that group as the source of any problems, which may or may not be correct. However, if you know they hold this opinion, you will have a better handle on the situation.

Spiral Notebook

For taking notes during the search and discovery process and during interviews with key implementation participants, the IC should use an ordinary spiral-bound notebook of any size that meets your personal preference. A loose-leaf binder is less suitable because pages can be torn out or disordered, impairing the book's functionality. When the IC starts on an implementation, she gets bombarded with more information than she can assimilate or absorb. So don't worry about organizing your spiral notebook. Just take notes fast and furiously. Gathering this information, like investigative reporting, is crucial to the implementation effort. Make notes to yourself about who is doing what, who has the power, and who has the most to win by implementing the system or product. You are a kind of cultural anthropologist gathering data for the good of the entire culture (maybe you'll be able to break them away from cannibalism). Figure 5.1 is an example of an IC's Spiral Notebook.

In the spiral notebook, draw a line across the page at the end of each conversation—for demarcation. Since these notes aren't organized, if you agree to do something, draw a big star next to that item in the spiral notebook. That way you can later quickly scan the book for "to do" or action items, helping you to follow through with what you said you'd do. In addition to the answers to the questions already outlined, the spiral notebook will contain these additional items in random order:

1. Generalized notes and impressions
2. Tasks you are committed to doing

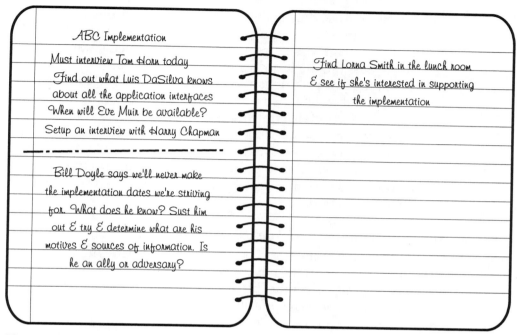

ABC Implementation

Must interview Tom Horn today

Find out what Luis DaSilva knows about all the application interfaces

When will Eve Muir be available?

Setup an interview with Harry Chapman

- - - - - - - - - - - - - - - - -

Bill Doyle says we'll never make the implementation dates we're striving for. What does he know? Just him out & try & determine what are his motives & sources of information. Is he an ally or adversary?

Find Lorna Smith in the lunch room & see if she's interested in supporting the implementation

Figure 5.1.   Spiral Notebook

3. The names of people someone said you should speak to
4. Commitments that people have made to you
5. Definitions of words or acronyms you don't understand

It's always a good idea to date and time stamp the notebook as often as you can remember to. And never take a page out of the spiral notebook; that way it will always be in chronological order. The most important thing is to keep writing!

JIP Implementation Kickoff Session

While you're feeling your way around an organization during search and discovery trying to figure out what needs to be done, you're also identifying everyone who has anything to do with the implementation. Once you've interviewed all the people you can identify as key to the implementation, you call for a JIP Implementation Kickoff Session and get all these people in one room. (Understand that you won't identify or meet some of the key people for some time because during the early stages of an implementation no one really understands who all the key players are.) The JIP Implementation Kickoff Session sets up the entire implementation effort. In this JIP Session, the IC presents the business case for implementing the system or product and gets agreement on what's the next major deliverable. She then proceeds to define tasks, determine responsibility, and detail a timeline for their completion. Since the JIP Implementation Kickoff Session is a high-level view of the implementation effort, a task usually impacts that group's deliverable. For example, Group A will produce the test data, Group B will develop a customer contact strategy, while Group C is responsible for resource acquisition.

JIP Implementation Kickoff Session
1. Tell *why* the system or product is being implemented.
2. Get *agreement* on the next major deliverable.
3. Define *what* tasks must be completed.
4. Determine *who* is responsible for these tasks.
5. Detail *when* these tasks must be done.

Concluding an Implementation Stage

One of the biggest issues in an implementation is how to conclude one stage and move on to the next. Usually everyone has a different opinion about when to move to the next major deliverable because they can't agree whether the current stage is complete or not. The IC's job is to get everyone to agree about what constitutes completion of a stage for this implementation, in this organization, under these circumstances. This is what everyone always wants to know: Are we there yet?

Do your own research and substantiate every claim you hear when trying to conclude a stage. Project Managers have been known to bring in an IC and hurry them to pick up the pace of the implementation. They're in a rush to say, "Programming is done and we're ready for integration testing." But you'll often find by checking around with the programmers that not only is the programming incomplete, there are also design issues still open. In this case, having open issues means the implementation isn't even out of the design stage yet. So don't always rush in where the Project Manager wants you to tread.

Developing an Implementation Plan

The Implementation Plan is developed in JIP Implementation Planning Sessions. After the IC has set the precepts and tone for the implementation with the JIP Implementation Kickoff Session, she calls for a JIP Implementation Planning Session. Based on her research from search and discovery, the IC invites those people she thinks should be making the decisions about the issues of the implementation. Some implementations are so large or complex that the IC has to hold JIP Preplanning Session(s) to organize the JIP Implementation Planning Session(s). The IC is responsible for providing all pertinent information and documentation to the participants prior to the JIP Sessions. Be thorough in organizing and structuring the JIP Implementation Planning Session so that the participants are given every chance to produce a comprehensive Implementation Plan in the time allotted.

Systemic View

When planning an implementation the IC must take the *systemic view* and look at the implementation in its relationship to all the other information systems within the organization. In too many projects, all the design effort is very low level and focused on detailed specifications even though the global-architectural issues haven't been addressed. The global-architectural issues are concerned with how all the complex, concurrent information technol-

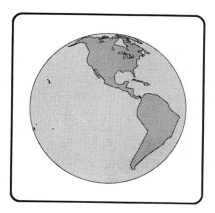

ogy within the organization interacts. In the information systems industry the telecommunications architecture usually has a systemic perspective because telecommunications address global issues within the hardware environment. However, inadequate global architecture is one of the problems endemic to the application systems because application programmers have always written programs for their own users and their own specialized requirements with no view toward the global realities. In order to implement a product or system, the IC must take a systemic view and integrate the implementation into all the other information systems within the organization.

The systemic view <u>perceives</u> the implementation as an integrated portion of the whole information systems environment.

Architecture of Systems

ICs find that many organizations have no policy or processes in place to deal with the growing issues of systems architecture, which refers to the overall design, interconnection, and interaction of the principal components of a system, or group of systems. Nevertheless, almost everyone in these organizations think they know a lot about architecture and are not shy about criticizing someone else's approach to working with the system's architecture. However, it's rare to find any good processes in place by which you can scope out what your implementation's architecture is or should be, or even an architectural standard by which it can be measured. This condition within the industry is made worse by the fact that architectural policy tends to change with changes in management and the latest theories on the street. While it certainly makes sense that the systems you're implementing be architecturally sound, ICs have to work within the realities of the organization. The IC's ultimate responsibility is to get *something* implemented. Sometimes you'll find you just can't get *anything* implemented without tackling the organization's architectural issues.

Having to take on an organization's policies or standards (or lack of same) is a sure prescription for massive personal and professional aggravation. Therefore, tackle only those architectural issues that are crucial to your implementation's success. Don't jeopardize your implementation by pressing on or pointing out architectural boondoggles not directly relevant to your effort. The penalty is to get sucked into infinitely regressive issues that you will never resolve, but will only regret.

Implementation Documentation

After several weeks of taking notes in the spiral notebook, you will find that it all starts to come together; you're able to go back through the spiral notebook and reread everything and begin to piece together the Implementation Workbook. The Implementation Workbook is described in detail in Chapter 6. You're now able to determine anything you might have missed, such as: Who haven't you talked to? What issues are still outstanding? What hasn't been done?

As the Implementation Plan matures, compile a loose-leaf bound Implementation Workbook that is well thought out and organized into sections of your choosing. You couldn't have possibly built a well-documented workbook when you first started because you didn't even know what stage the implementation was in, what the issues were, or what needed to be done. Figure 5.2 is an example of an Implementation Workbook.

Figure 5.2.   **Implementation Workbook**

The Spiral Notebook has a limited life. Once you get the implementation rolling you will rarely look at it again. But when you are starting out, it's an invaluable tool for just straight-ahead information gathering. At that point, you couldn't possibly *filter* all the information that's coming at you, each time saying, "This is a question and that belongs on the question page. And this is a to-do item and that goes on the action item page." When you can't filter it, just take it! Later you will cull through your spiral notebook again and again to organize your thoughts and determine what's to be done. Once you're organized and have a framework for understanding the implementation and who all the players are, then you can begin to efficiently organize and build the Implementation Workbook. The Implementation Workbook is described in Chapter 6.

Implementation Contact List

It's important to build an Implementation Contact List. From day one, start gathering names, titles, phone numbers, e-mail addresses, mail-stop codes, and brief descriptions of what these people mean to the implementation. Keep updating your contact list throughout the life of the implementation and publish it for dissemination. You can start a contact list on the last page of your spiral notebook, and later expand and convert it into a more readable format that is put into the Implementation Workbook. In the beginning, grab everyone's name and number because you don't know who's a player in your implementation and who isn't. As the implementation goes forward you can edit and refine your contact list. Figure 5.3 is an example of an Implementation Contact List. Freely distribute your contact list to anyone and everyone to promote communication and coordination within the implementation.

A Day in the Life

Many times ICs get called in only after an implementation is already in trouble or is late getting started, so there may be real tension in the air. For the first time, people are starting to address the implementation issues. There are always people on any project who are doing some part of the IC job. But normally it isn't their only responsibility so they are delighted when an IC arrives on the scene

ABC Implementation
Contact List As Of MM/DD/YY

Name	Division	E-Mail ID	Org #	Pager #	Home #

Figure 5.3. **Implementation Contact List**

to alleviate their burden. You'll find these people are usually more than willing to offload onto you, the IC, with useful stuff like: here's what you need to know, here's everything we've done to date, here's everything we haven't done, and here's what we wanted to do but never got finished. Good luck.

CHAPTER 6

Planning the Implementation: Accommodating Uniqueness

For an implementation to be successful the *implementation planning* must accommodate "uniqueness." Despite what many information systems industry pundits say, implementations are not all the same. While there are many similarities among implementations, there are also as many differences. People who repeatedly conform to the same implementation routines get trapped in those procedures, which are based on previous implementations that may have little in common with the current one. They fail to realize the gizmo or procedure that meant salvation on the last implementation may not even be appropriate for this implementation. They end up proving their procedure instead of coordinating the implementation in all its dynamic diversity. Remember that every implementation is unique. Keep your eyes and ears open; every implementation is an opportunity to learn something new.

> *Implementing information systems is an exercise in complex inter-relationships, both human and technological.*

BROADCASTING THE IMPLEMENTATION

As a precursor to any implementation planning, the Implementation Coordinator and the Project Manager must "broadcast" their implementation. The IC sees to it that their implementation is scheduled on

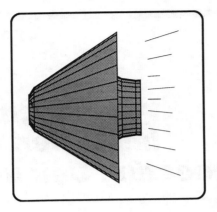

each group's staff meeting calendar as an agenda item. The IC and the Project Manager attend these groups' staff meetings and tell them about the implementation. They alert them to the fact that this implementation is coming, its approximate dates, its projected demands (in terms of resources required from that group), and how the IC and Project Manager think the implementation will impact that group's area. The goal is to make sure that each group can't pretend it's never heard about the implementation. If, over the course of the implementation, any new information turns up that will be of significance to any of these groups, the IC again gets scheduled on that particular group's staff-meeting calendar as an agenda item and presents these findings. The IC takes a proactive role to ensure that her needs are going to be met and that the services she requires of others in the organization will be available for the implementation. Here's a typical list of groups that need to know:

- Data Center(s) Group
- Telecommunications Group
- Systems Programming Group
- Storage Management Group
- Quality Assurance Group
- Application Programming Group(s)
- Database Administration Group

An IC can never assume that she will get everyone's cooperation for the implementation. She knows going into the implementation that she must confer with everyone and make completely certain that she has their cooperation. An implementation is headed for trouble when a plan is written and dates are chosen without getting the other participating and interfacing groups' OK and assurances of their support. Broadcasting the implementation is the first step in making sure that every person and group is aware of the implementation, and that their support will be forthcoming and on schedule. If you don't get everyone's support for your implementation then you will end up dragging them along, kicking and screaming.

IMPLEMENTATION PLAN

The Implementation Plan is the most current statement of the work to be done to implement the system or product. The Implementation Plan is developed in JIP Implementation Planning Sessions. JIP Implementation Planning Sessions are described in detail later in this chapter. In your particular Implementation Plan you must decide the type and number of documents required to best state the work to be done. Here is a list of the documents that would be found in a prototypical Implementation Plan:

- Deliverables Document
- Work Statements
- Sign-Off Sheets
- Schedule
- Test Plan
- Implementation Management Teams

* * *

- Problem Log
- Problem Reports
- Change Log
- Change Request
- Configuration Management

* * *

- Implementation Resource Requirements
- Customer-Contact Strategy
- Training

Deliverables Document

The *Deliverables Document* outlines what *decisions* have been reached in the JIP Sessions and what *deliverables* have been promised. The Deliverables Document restates the Task Log with more detail than the cursory who, what, and when of the Task Log. The Deliverables Document is written by the IC and is usually for her reference only.

Work Statements

Work Statements are written by each group and/or person involved in the implementation, and define in detail the deliverables for which they are responsible. As Work Statements are formulated and written, the author or authors are forced to become clear and precise. Generating a Work Statement is a reporting process that debugs the thinking of the person who writes it. The Work Statement also clarifies any ambiguity that may exist between the producers and recipients of deliverables. If someone or some group doesn't write a Work Statement then they can never be held accountable for anything. ICs have witnessed ugly situations because implementation participants did not produce a Work Statement, and then "when the whip comes down," those without Work Statements denied any culpability. To avoid this scenario, always get a Work Statement from every person and group listed on the Task Log. If there is a problem with some person or group refusing to write a Work Statement, the IC should escalate the issue to ensure compliance. Figure 6.1 is an example of a Work Statement.

Sign-Off Sheets

Sign-Off Sheets are in effect contracts that formalize the acceptance of deliverables by the person or persons responsible for receiving them. If the sign offs are conducted at a public venue such as a JIP Session, the signers are tacitly implying to the organization at large that they support this implementation. Those persons ultimately accountable for the system or product to be implemented have to sign off on the Implementation Plan. However, you may find that Sign-Off Sheets for some particular aspect of the implementation may also be appropriate. For example, you might want to get the business users to sign off on the deliverables for the User Acceptance Test (described in Chapter 7) at a JIP Session. Then later they won't be able to say, "Oh, that isn't what I thought you intended to

```
                    Work Statement

   Implementation:                    Date:

   Prepared By:
           Phone Number:          E-Mail ID:

   Application:

   Division:          Group:          Team:
        Division Manager:
             Phone Number:        E-Mail ID:
        Group Manager:
             Phone Number:        E-Mail ID:
        Team Leader:
             Phone Number:        E-Mail ID:

   Personnel Committed To The Implementation Effort.
        Name:
             Phone Number:        E-Mail ID:
        Name:
             Phone Number:        E-Mail ID:
                                *
                                *
                                *
   Resources Required:
   (hardware, software, tech support, contractors, etc.)


   Statement Of The Work To Be Done:
```

Figure 6.1. **Work Statement**

deliver." It's OK if they balk when the test results are delivered, as long as they've signed off on *what was* to be delivered. If they want the test results reconstituted, then they will have to buy you the time to do this, instead of your having to go nuts trying to produce something they want at the eleventh hour because it was left unspecified early on. Figure 6.2 is an example of a Sign-Off Sheet.

Schedule

The *Schedule* shows the times and dates that each deliverable within the Implementation Plan must be accomplished. It's always good to

```
ABC Implementation                    Sign-Up Request

Mr. Getit Done                            January 22, 1994
ABC Implementation Coordinator

Please  review  the  ABC Implementation Plan  and sign below
indicating  your  support  for  the  implementation  and your
commitment  of  resources  for  the    completion of   the ABC
Implementation.  Your sign-up is needed by February 7, 1995.
If you have any reservations regarding the impact of the ABC
Implementation in your area that would inhibit your sign-up,
please   contact the Implementation Coordinator Getit Done at
phone number, e-mail ID, or pager number.
```

	NAME	SIGNATURE	DATE
1.			
2.			
3.			
4.			
5.			
6.			
7.			
8.			
9.			
10.			
11.			
12.			

Figure 6.2.   **Sign-Off Sheet**

have graphical representations of the timeline with either Gantt charts or histograms. People appreciate it when they can see the deliverables mapped against dates and times. Figure 6.3 is an example of an Implementation Schedule with the deliverables (i.e., tasks) and corresponding dates graphically represented.

Test Plan

The implementation *Test Plan* can be as large as, and for some implementations is even larger than, the Implementation Plan it-

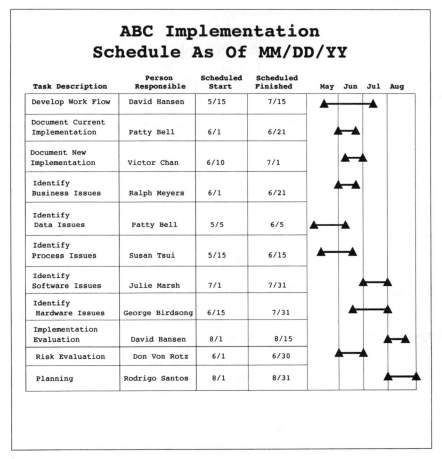

**ABC Implementation
Schedule As Of MM/DD/YY**

Task Description	Person Responsible	Scheduled Start	Scheduled Finished	May	Jun	Jul	Aug
Develop Work Flow	David Hansen	5/15	7/15				
Document Current Implementation	Patty Bell	6/1	6/21				
Document New Implementation	Victor Chan	6/10	7/1				
Identify Business Issues	Ralph Meyers	6/1	6/21				
Identify Data Issues	Patty Bell	5/5	6/5				
Identify Process Issues	Susan Tsui	5/15	6/15				
Identify Software Issues	Julie Marsh	7/1	7/31				
Identify Hardware Issues	George Birdsong	6/15	7/31				
Implementation Evaluation	David Hansen	8/1	8/15				
Risk Evaluation	Don Von Rotz	6/1	6/30				
Planning	Rodrigo Santos	8/1	8/31				

Figure 6.3.   Implementation Schedule

self. The Test Plan is developed in JIP Test Planning Sessions and is described in detail in Chapter 7.

Implementation Management Teams

The *Implementation Management Teams* administer the logistical problems of implementing the system or product. Documented in the Implementation Plan is each team's duties, who is on the team, and each person's role and responsibilities. These Implementation Management Teams are described in detail in Chapter 8. The following are types of Implementation Management Teams:

- Installation Management Team
- Problem Report Team
- Problem Management Team
- Change Management Team

Tools

Any *tools* used in the implementation effort should be described in the Implementation Plan with templates or examples when applicable. For example, the tools the Implementation Management Teams will use should be documented. These tools are described in detail in Chapter 8. The following are the different Implementation Planning Tools:

- Problem Log
- Problem Reports
- Change Log
- Change Request
- Configuration Management

Implementation Resource Requirements

The *Implementation Resource Requirements* document is used by the IC to budget every resource required by the implementation. These resources could be personnel, software, hardware, party favors, and so forth. Whatever is needed for the implementation to succeed should be included in the Implementation Resource Requirements document. The Implementation Resource Requirements are developed in JIP Implementation Planning Sessions and the document is included in the Implementation Plan. Figure 6.4 is an example of an Implementation Resource Requirements Document.

Customer-Contact Strategy

For some implementations the IC is supposed to conduct JIP Sessions to facilitate the development of a *Customer-Contact Strategy*. This strategy should be documented and included in the Implementation Plan. In JIP Customer-Contact Strategy Sessions, the participants figure out how the sales representatives (or whomever) are going to talk to the customers about the system or product to be implemented. The session participants also need to come to some agreement about what they are going to say to the organization's representatives, who will in turn talk to customers about the new

**ABC Implementation
Resource Requirements Document
As Of MM/DD/YY**

Resource Description	Date Required	Person Requesting	Person Approving	Estimated Cost

Figure 6.4.   Implementation Resource Requirements Document

system or product. There can potentially be many customer-contact points within most organizations that could be called upon to talk about a new system or product. Therefore, the JIP Customer-Contact Strategy Session participants need to figure out where all the customer-contact points are, and what the representatives at these contact points should know and say.

Training

Training (sometimes referred to as "technology transfer") and the documentation that supports it are important issues for every implementation and should always be part of your Implementation Plan. Any training required is developed in JIP Training Strategy Sessions. ICs set up training for all users whose environment will be changed as a result of the system or product being implemented. It's also an excellent idea to set up training for the management personnel whose areas will be impacted by the implemented system or product. While these managers won't necessarily need hands-on training with the new system, they still need to learn and understand why and how the structure of their organization is being changed. The importance of this instruction is not to be minimized. If management doesn't understand the idea(s) behind the changes, they will never completely support the new system, and ultimately this can be devastating to the implementation. Needless to say, it's never easy to get management to come to training or even informational JIP Sessions, but the ultimate success of your implementation may depend on it.

IMPLEMENTATION WORKBOOK

The Implementation Workbook serves as the repository of all information relative to the implementation. It is the benchmark by which all implementation activities are judged. As a communication device the workbook ensures that every effort expended on the implementation is grounded in the same shared and understood precepts. Since the Implementation Workbook is the basis for implementation control, it's imperative to keep it as up-to-date as possible, and adapt it to reflect the changing circumstances of the implementation. As the steward of the Implementation Workbook the IC must make sure all implementation documentation is contained therein. For example, if someone must file a form with the quality assurance group, you get a copy of that form and include it in the Implementation Workbook. The workbook is maintained in a loose-leaf binder that for large or complex implementations may expand to several individual binders.

What's Included in the Implementation Workbook:
1. Contact List
2. Issues Log
3. Task Log
4. JIP Session Notes
5. Implementation Plan
6. Interface Specification Documents

7. Status Reports
8. Glossary

The *Contact List* is a compilation of every implementation participant's name, title, phone number, e-mail addresses, organizational mail-stop, etc. The Contact List is described in detail in Chapter 5.

The *Issues Log* enumerates every issue that is in dispute or unresolved. The Issues Log is the responsibility of the IC and is described in detail in Chapter 4.

The *Task Log* specifies who is responsible for each implementation task and is described in detail in Chapter 4.

The *JIP Session Notes* are a written report of what happened in a particular JIP Session. This report is always distributed to the attendees of the JIP Session and should also be included in the Implementation Workbook. The JIP Session Notes are described in detail in Chapter 4.

The *Implementation Plan* is a document that details what must be done to implement the system or product. The Implementation Plan is described in detail earlier in this chapter.

An *Interface Specification Document* (ISD) is produced by each group that interfaces with the new system or product, and outlines what each must do to support the implementation. The JIP ISD is described in detail later in this chapter.

Status Reports

A *Status Report* is a brief written synopsis of a group's or a person's efforts to date. The report details what was accomplished, what wasn't accomplished, and what are the open issues and concerns. The Status Report is verbally presented at the regular JIP Status Session and a copy is given to the IC for inclusion in the Implementation Workbook. Status Reports are described in detail in Chapter 8.

Glossary

The IC should maintain a running *Glossary* of the terms and expressions used and developed during the implementation, and document them with definitions in the Implementation Workbook. Language as we use it in everyday conversation is in a constant process of change with regard to the way it sounds and what it means. In the information systems industry, both nomenclature and usage are mutating and evolving even more rapidly. Not only does the IC have to deal with the nomenclature of the technology in the information systems industry, but she also has to deal with the idiosyncratic nuances of the language as used in her particular organization. It's essential to the success of the implementation that everyone communicate from a common and shared understanding. Therefore, the Glossary codifies and standardizes the definition of terms and expressions used during the implementation, ensuring that everyone is speaking the same "language." Figure 6.5 is an example of an Implementation Glossary.

ABC Implementation Glossary As Of MM/DD/YY

Terms & Expressions	Definition	Meaning
OFD	out for the day	they're gone
RIF	reduction in force	loss of resources
SLA	service level agreement	allowable down-time
SOB	Sales Order Billing	billing system
SOE	Service Order Entry	order entry system
TBD	to be determined	not now

Figure 6.5.   Glossary

JIP PLANNING AND DESIGN SESSIONS

The JIP Planning and Design Sessions are the forums at which everything relative to the implementation of the system or product is hashed out and mapped out. There are numerous other JIP Sessions, but the Planning and Design Sessions are where all the formative work of the implementation is done.

Types of JIP Planning and Design Sessions:
1. Preplanning
2. Implementation Planning
3. Contingency Planning
4. Test Planning
5. Interface Design

JIP Preplanning Sessions

The JIP Implementation Planning Session is where the Implementation Plan is built. However, some implementations are so large or complex that the IC must hold one or more JIP Preplanning Sessions to develop an agenda and schedule for the full-blown JIP Implementation Planning Session. At the JIP Preplanning Session the IC tells the managers from the applicable areas, "Here's what I want to accomplish in the JIP Implementation Planning Session, so who is the right person from your group to participate?" Typically it isn't the manager, it's the technical specialist with the expertise in that particular area. The managers will tell you who these people are. Then the IC asks, "OK, who's the backup if this person falls ill?" because it's necessary to get a secondary person for assignment from each group. The IC makes it very clear to the managers in the JIP Preplanning Session that she is going to conduct a JIP Implementation Planning Session that may take one or more days depending on the implementation. If the key resources (technical specialists) from their groups are not in attendance, then the entire JIP Session will be a waste of everyone's time. So the IC makes sure these managers commit to having their technical specialists at the JIP Implementation Planning Session, right there in the JIP Preplanning Session! If a manager makes that commitment in front of all the other managers it will be difficult for her to backslide later and say something else came up.

Coverage

Coverage is the concept that the key resources (responsible professionals) the IC needs in attendance at a JIP Session will in fact be at that JIP Session. Each group must have someone at the JIP Session who's responsible for the coverage of their issues. Ensuring that every area has coverage for the JIP Session can be a constant source of aggravation for the IC.

The IC must negotiate with managers to get the right person sent to the JIP Implementation Planning Session. Sometimes you must make a preemptive challenge: "No, Joe Montana would not be OK. He attended one of the previous JIP Sessions and obviously did not understand the implementation issues or problems. He then wrote a terrible summation of what your group would have to do to support the implementation." If you've done your search and discovery well, you may be able to suggest someone else within that group whom you have already checked out personally or who others recommended would be a good player to send to the JIP Implementation Planning Session.

JIP Implementation Planning Sessions

The JIP Implementation Planning Session is the forum at which the IC facilitates the development of an Implementation Plan as a cooperative effort amongst every group involved with the implementation. The IC makes sure that every aspect of the Implementation Plan is addressed in the JIP Implementation Planning Session(s).

Once upon an implementation, the IC had a manager call and say, "We really don't have anyone we can assign to a whole-day JIP Implementation Planning Session. You know, you aren't even on our calendar for six more months, so we aren't even going to assign anyone to your implementation effort until that time." The IC let them have it. "Hey, I hate to rain on your parade, but I need your participation now even though your deliverable isn't due for six months. Check it out: I'm only asking for one day, and it's *important* that someone responsible for your group attend the JIP Session." At this point the manager said, "Well, ex-cu-se me! Maybe you could give me an agenda stating the times that particular topics will be discussed. Then I'd know when to send my programmer along so she won't have to devote an entire day to the JIP Session." The IC responded, "Not so fast. I'm not about to tell you what hours we're going to discuss which topics because even I don't know that."

The IC didn't want to publish a detailed agenda because she knew it would be tough to predict with any certainty how long the topics would take, or when supplemental issues would surface that might be important to the group. The manager then said, "You're tough. Suppose we send one person in the morning and another in the afternoon?" The IC said that was OK, but pointed out to the manager that it was the responsibility of those two people to get together (over lunch, if necessary) to bridge any information gaps between the morning and afternoon JIP Sessions. The IC isn't required to bring the afternoon person "up to speed" on issues discussed in the morning, and it would be an imposition on the other participants, wasting their valuable time and assaulting their boredom threshold.

Every IC invariably has her own ideas about what will and will not work, and a gut sense about whether "That sounds good" or "That doesn't sound good." However, ICs try to avoid forming any preconceived notions about how the implementation planning should go. ICs are committed to letting the participants of the JIP Implementation Planning Session *plan* the implementation while they *facilitate* that planning effort. When discussing the implementation, everyone spews forth ideas, which the Scribe duly notes on the Session Boards. The participants devise strategies for how they are going to do it, what is going to happen on which day, and who is going to be accountable for what. The bottom line is that people determine for themselves who is responsible for each task. For example, the IC knows there must be an escalation plan, but it's much more effective if the JIP Session participants themselves say, "Hey, we need an escalation plan." Then, with the IC's facilitation, they proceed to develop one—but with more commitment than if the IC had directly instigated or forced it.

JIP Contingency Planning Session

JIP Contingency Planning Sessions are forums in which contingency plans for the implementation are developed. An IC is always thinking, "What bugs and other little things out there could impede the implementation?" The IC facilitates the development of strategies in JIP Contingency Planning Sessions in order to accommodate anything that might happen. (Of course, because *Murphy lives*, you can't imagine everything that might possibly happen!) Also, there is obviously a price/impact ratio in effect here. If something is prohibitively expensive to protect against and its impact upon the implementation effort is minimal, then it's not worth developing a contingency. The real value of proactively developing contingencies through JIP Sessions is that you can just refer to the contingency script when something does happen and take the appropriate action, instead of extemporizing, as Indiana Jones did when the giant stone ball of doom rolled down toward him.

Don't worry. I'll think of something.

—Indiana Jones

Developing Contingencies

The value of developing contingencies will seem particularly evident when you find yourself in a situation where you have five days to correct a problem and the solution has a 60-day lead time. You can't afford to get trapped like that because of its impact on your implementation. You also can't be unrealistic and say, "I've restructured your 60-day lead time into five days because I've got this little problem." No one may be able to control that lead time because, for example, it may take two months to order and install a piece of key equipment. Or what if you get a directive from senior management to conduct an organization-wide systems test, and that test uses all the systems resources? Or what if equipment problems cause a lack of capacity in the test environment that prevents the application groups from getting their testing done? When doing contingency planning, it may be helpful to recall any problems you've had before with this particular organization, because they may well recur.

> The excuse that there is a lack of testing resources always contains a touch of irony because the implementors are treated as outsiders trying to break in, when in fact they are insiders trying to get something implemented! Lack of testing resources is also frustrating because hardware is cheap. The real expense in systems development and implementation is the labor.

If It Becomes a Problem

The phrase, "If it becomes a problem . . ." should be anathema to an IC. Although fixing problems "on the fly" in most cases is possible, you're usually treating the symptom, not the disease. When you implement changes to correct a symptom and don't address its root cause, you're creating more problems in the long run than you solved with the quick fix. Fixing problems on the fly tends to degrade the quality of the system or product being implemented by impacting its operational effectiveness.

ICs who have worked in organizations that operate under the "If it becomes a problem . . ." scenario know that this is like saying, "When we run out of capacity let's discuss funding for more hardware." Organizations such as these experience considerable difficulty with their implementations because they don't proactively take the approach of developing contingency plans. ICs are always asking, "Why does it have to become a problem? Can't we devise a solution now?" ICs plan for the unplannable by defining and preparing for every contingency.

Once upon an implementation, the IC had a situation in which she was facilitating the JIP Contingency Planning Session and one of the participating applications said all their testing was based on the assumption that another implementation scheduled ahead of theirs would in fact be installed without incident. But if the other implementation failed, then their testing strategy would be invalid because the code on which it was based would not be in the production environment. The IC documented that constraint in the Implementation Plan and then pushed to develop a contingency plan in the event of failure by the preceding implementation.

This anecdote exemplifies a classic case in which the IC could have sloughed off by saying, "If it becomes a problem . . . then we'll think of something." Instead, she told the JIP Contingency Planning Session participants, "We're not going to get caught with our pants down on this one, folks. What can we do to plan for this situation ahead of time, just in case?" This IC then facilitated a contingency plan.

JIP Test Planning Sessions

The JIP Test Planning Sessions are forums in which the Implementation Test Plan is defined, developed, and documented. The JIP Test Planning Sessions are described in detail in Chapter 7.

JIP Interface Design Sessions

JIP Interface Design Sessions are forums in which every interface created by the system or product being implemented is defined. Although different systems or applications are obviously going to interface with one another, the ergonomics of the human-computer interface also need to be resolved. Many interfacing issues are typically handled in Joint Application Development (JAD) Sessions. However, there are always some issues that need to be resolved in JIP Interface Design Sessions, such as technical problems that become evident over the life of the development effort, or the ergonomics of the system or product.

The IC doesn't let the JIP Interface Design Session delve into explicit interfacing issues among two or three applications because almost everyone else in attendance would probably lose interest and feel their time was being wasted. Instead, the IC logs the item as an interfacing issue, identifies which groups need to work on that problem, and then instructs those groups to work it out amongst themselves. Later they can let the IC know what they came up with. If these groups request it, or if the IC perceives the need, the IC can facilitate a JIP Working Session for just these few groups to work out their interfacing issues. The point of the JIP Interface Design Session is to identify all the interfaces, document which groups are designated to work on those interfaces, and log all the interfacing issues in the Issues Log.

An _interface_ is that point at which independent or diverse systems interact.

JIP Interface Specification Document

The JIP Interface Specification Document (ISD) details what an application or system that has one or more interfaces, as a result of the system or product to be implemented, must do to support the interface(s). The IC requests a JIP Interface Specification Document from the groups and/or persons on both sides of every implementation interface. Obviously, in some situations this document could be a one-liner. For example, "Group A is going to pass us the time-and-date stamp (24 hour notation and Julian format) that we need to process our transactions." However, it's still important to document every component of each interface. Figure 6.6 is an example of a JIP Interface Specification Document.

Every group directly supporting the implementation, and even

```
              JIP Interface Specification Document

   Implementation:                          Date:

   Prepared By:
           Phone Number:              E-Mail ID:

   Application:

   Interfacing Systems:
      Upstream Applications or Servers:



      Downstream Applications or Clients:



   Statement Of What You Plan To Deliver
        To The Other System(s):



   Statement Of What You Expect To Receive
        From The Other System(s):
```

Figure 6.6.   JIP Interface Specification Document

those groups indirectly impacted by the implementation should produce a JIP ISD. The IC budgets for a technical writer in the Implementation Resource Requirements so that each group ends up with a "good-looking" JIP Interface Specification Document. ICs find that it encourages people to do their JIP ISD right if they know a technical writer is going to produce a finished product from their work. Upon completion, the JIP Interface Specification Documents are distributed to the implementation participants and the IC maintains all of them in the Implementation Workbook. Periodically the

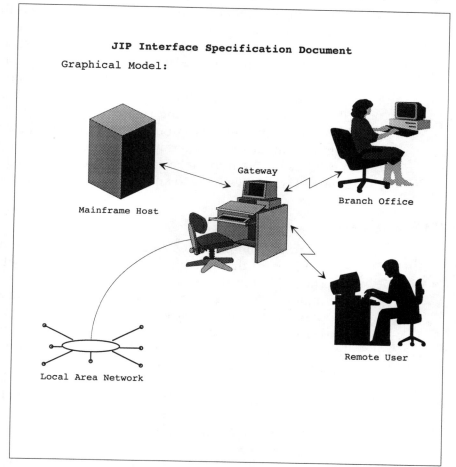

Figure 6.7. **JIP ISD Graphical Model**

IC reviews the documents for conformity among the groups' interfacing specifications.

Each JIP Interface Specification Document should also contain a *graphical model* depicting every interface referenced in that document. Such a model makes it much easier for everyone to see how and where their particular interface (or interfaces) intersect and interact with those of the producers of the document. Figure 6.7 is an example of a JIP ISD Graphical Model.

Each JIP Interface Specification Document is a communication vehicle (to the other group or groups with which the authoring group is interfacing), letting them know what the authors are going to *give* them and also what the authors *expect* from them. If each group doesn't update their JIP ISD, then there will be some untruths being circulated around the organization. ICs strongly suggest to every group that they "stay on top of" their JIP ISDs and keep updating them with any new information. Although ICs usually don't have authority over these groups, they can still tell them that if they don't update their JIP Interface Specification Documents then the burden is on them to make sure that the interfacing group(s) are aware of what they need to know.

JIP Walk Throughs

Every group that produces a JIP Interface Specification Document should present that document at a JIP Walk Through with all the interfacing applications and any other participants of the implementation who might choose to attend. If, during the JIP Walk Through, questions are raised and things are unclear, the IC logs those issues on the Issues Log. When the group republishes their JIP Interface Specification Document, the IC can then review the updated document to make sure it addresses and satisfactorily resolves all the issues raised in the JIP Walk Through. It isn't always necessary to have another JIP Walk Through, especially if the issues raised were trivial. However, if the JIP Interface Specification Document has major problems, than another JIP Walk Through is probably appropriate.

ICs always strive for a lot of exposure in JIP Walk Throughs, which means inviting managers and getting them involved. This has two benefits: it gives impetus to those participants who aren't playing at the same level to get up to speed, and it gives people a chance to show off their work. The walk through becomes the presenter's JIP Session and personal turn to shine. It's important that management attend the JIP Walk Throughs because they bear the responsibility for the organization's information systems. In JIP Walk Throughs with only technical specialists in attendance, decisions can be made that many managers would question on the grounds that they were against "standard industry practice" or organizational policy. Therefore, it's best if the programmers and other technical specialists are made to conform to managerial standards and overview, and are not allowed to extemporaneously tweak or "kluge" the system or product to be implemented. By attending the JIP Walk Throughs, management personnel can make sure this doesn't happen.

Sometimes a group doesn't really need to walk through their JIP Interface Specification Document with the other implementation groups because their interface with the other groups is minimal and they feed no downstream applications. However, what ICs find is that such groups, who aren't core to the implementation, may voluntarily approach them and say, "When can we walk through our JIP Interface Specification Document?" ICs gladly acknowledge these requests and schedule JIP Walk Throughs for them also.

Once upon an implementation, the IC scheduled a JIP Walk Through of a JIP Interface Specification Document with the approval of the programming group's manager. The JIP Walk Through was attended by the business user who was going to own the system to be implemented, the programmers who produced the JIP Interface Specification Document, the programming group's manager, and the programming group's senior manager. But the JIP Interface Specification Document was incomplete and poorly documented. It had been "thrown together" by the programmers, had been given a sloppy "once-over" by the technical writer, and was now being presented without rewrite or consideration. The programming group's senior manager was visibly upset, and after the JIP Walk Through reassigned the programming group's manager to other projects. The IC was delighted. The JIP Walk Through had proven to be a good forum for accountability. Nothing the IC could have said would ever have had the impact of that poorly prepared JIP Interface Specification Document that was presented in the JIP Walk Through.

Senior Management Checkpoints

ICs usually provide opportunities for senior-level management to review the implementation effort. ICs do this by putting checkpoints in the Implementation Plan for the senior managers (executive vice-presidents, senior vice-presidents, etc.) who are interested in the implementation. A checkpoint is typically a JIP Walk Through to which the senior manager is invited. The IC lets the group making the presentation know that their senior manager will

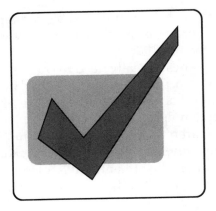

attend. ICs find that once they have announced that the senior manager will be attending the JIP Walk Through, they invariably start getting requests for additional people to be placed on the JIP Walk Through distribution list, and for extra copies of the applicable implementation documentation. What happens is that the group to be reviewed starts to educate their management and senior manager so that when the JIP Walk Through is held, they will be able to get everyone's sign-off. The visibility provided by the attendance of senior management at JIP Walk Throughs really helps the credibility of the implementation and motivates each group to get their implementation effort organized.

IMPLEMENTING THE PLAN

On the front-end of the implementation, tasks may typically take weeks or even months. But getting closer to implementation, you'll find that you can break the Implementation Plan into smaller and smaller chunks. Tasks can now take hours and sometimes even minutes. JIP Implementation Planning Sessions are called throughout all stages of the implementation. There are always issues to be resolved and plans to be refined. In these JIP Sessions closer to the "implementation hour," the tasks can be segmented into subroutines requiring only hours and minutes.

Implementation Risk

The risks to which an organization is exposed as a result of an implementation can never be eliminated. However, risks can be managed if they can be identified. In every organization, ICs find there is always some resistance to addressing the risks and their implications. Unfortunately, a lack of willingness to discuss risk does not reduce the likelihood of those risks becoming serious problems. The IC facilitates discussions in JIP Sessions that identify the risks posed by an implementation. Identifying these risks provides an opportunity to better coordinate the implementation and minimizes the implementation's potentially negative impact upon the organization.

Time Management

Much of the time allotted to an implementation effort is spent in developing the different plans and resolving issues that necessarily arise. The actual "work" of the implementation is like the frosting on the cake. This can be tough on old-style managers who want to know why their technical specialists are in JIP Sessions when they feel they should be "working." However, by spending adequate time on the planning stages, you can substantially compress the actual work of the implementation and eliminate duplication of effort. After the planning is complete, ICs suggest dedicating however many people it takes to get the work done in two to three weeks. The value of this approach is that it dramatically reduces human errors in communication processes.

> *Measure your cloth seven times, for you only get to cut it once.*
>
> —*Russian Proverb*

When you compress the work of the implementation, you're left with plenty of time for testing. The robustness and reliability of the implemented product or system is determined by the types and amount of testing performed. It's hard to imagine doing too much implementation testing.

Dealing with Planning Difficulties

If each group involved in the implementation will just look after its own needs while the IC makes sure each group is systematically involved in the implementation planning, then most aspects of the implementation are probably covered. The IC's job gets tough in organizations whose personnel don't really understand what their jobs are and therefore can't focus on their appropriate functions. When people don't understand their roles or the extent of their responsibility, this inevitably causes corporate inertia—a prevalent malaise that afflicts many large organizations. In organizations whose personnel roles and responsibilities are not clearly defined, ICs find it difficult to get any planning accomplished, and even harder to get anything implemented!

Funding

How a project is funded can have a dramatic impact on implementation planning. Sometimes a business user wants the biggest component of a new system implemented first in order to justify the funding for the rest of the project. This runs counter to the principle of going low risk with the first stage of the implementation. If you implement a small piece of the system first, you can debug your Implementation Plan. Doing the biggest piece of an implementation first is very risky and can kill the entire project, not to mention your own budding career.

No Requirements

Most projects begin with the development of a User Requirements Document. However, there are projects in which the organization can achieve a more expedient implementation by exploiting technology rather than by developing detailed requirements. Building

Once upon an implementation, a new system was going to be implemented county-by-county around the state. The IC campaigned to initially implement one of the smaller counties in the state, but the Project Manager wanted to implement the biggest county (eight million people) first. His rationale was that by implementing the biggest county first, they could make a big impression on senior management and get lots of additional resources (dollars and personnel) for the rest of the implementation. There was no real way to effectively test every aspect of the Implementation Plan except to go "live," so that's what they did. The implementation crashed, and the implementation turned into a disaster that almost put the company out of business. Afterwards, while surveying the wreckage, the Project Manager said, "Wow, what a bad idea that was! Next time I'll listen to my IC's advice."

Once upon an implementation, the effort involved 6,000 intelligent workstations scattered throughout several states. The workstations served a number of different types of users such as businesses, residences, and schools. Determining the requirements was difficult with that many users, worsened by the fact that these users had no single spokesperson or proponent within the organization. As a result, there was no one the IC could ask, "How do you want to resolve this issue?" The IC continually got mixed messages from the steering committee that was trying to determine whether the user's needs were being met. The steering committee was itself staffed by people unfamiliar with information systems and therefore incapable of developing any requirements. It was also not in the steering committee's charter to develop user requirements. For this project, attempting to develop requirements was never going to shorten the time to implementation. And with no requirements, the only thing the IC could do was begin the implementation based on her own and the Project Manager's best judgment.

By implementing *something*, the IC got a lagging project jump-started, and forced the business users to get involved with evaluating what did and did not work. Projects with no requirements can still succeed by employing the strategy of incremental implementation and then evaluating the results.

an elaborate User Requirements Document presupposes that somebody (anybody) knows what is going on, and there are times when this just isn't the case. Going forward with the implementation of some portion of the system will at least initiate the process of actually determining what will (and will not) work.

Incremental Implementation

Incrementally implementing a system or product and then evaluating the results is the best approach for some projects. Sometimes too many unknowns militate against preparing a detailed Implementation Plan in advance. When you are on the "leading edge"—blending technologies to implement a new system—you're at the mercy of vendors who always overstate the capabilities of their products. This is a situation in which it pays to "start small," and then move forward incrementally while testing the leading edges. It's the only way to find out if the technologies are adequate for the job.

> Once upon an implementation, the IC coordinated the incremental implementation of a system in which the organization was able to determine that the type of routers necessary to meet their throughput requirements on the network would be prohibitively expensive. As a result, the entire project had to be reconstituted. For this implementation, capacity planning wasn't possible because the production environment couldn't be duplicated. So the only way to determine whether the architecture and technologies would work was via incremental implementation combined with evaluation.

THE COMPONENTS OF PLANNING

The components of planning are the tools, techniques, and "conventional wisdom" that is applied to the process of planning an implementation.

Applying Methodologies

A methodology is an orderly formulation of policies and procedures applied to the design, construction, and implementation of an information system. Although a methodology can be enormously valuable by providing a logical schematic for the development of systems, it should not become a rigid standard to be followed zealously. ICs witness implementations in which the Project Manager wants to follow the organization's methodology slavishly, with absolutely no spontaneity or creativity on the part of the implementation's participants. The danger in this approach is that it can degenerate into a scenario in which the implementors support the methodology instead of the methodology supporting the implementation. Every implementation has its own unique aspects and the implementors need to be allowed to use their creativity to dynamically respond to these situations. When it becomes necessary to deviate from the organization's methodology, the IC can write a business brief describing the situation and justifying why the deviation was warranted. In this way, the underlying precepts of the methodology can be upheld and the IC won't be branded as a rebel without a causative.

Once upon an implementation, the IC worked for an organization that employed a methodology that broke every task into "design, code, test, and implement," regardless of the nature of that task. This proved to be unwieldy during the implementation because many legitimate tasks, which sometimes took days and numerous people to resolve, did not fit into this paradigm. Therefore, the IC had no way to accommodate these tasks within the methodology's structure. The classic example involves tasks of "search and discovery," which are concerned with resolving issues and/or verifying assumptions. For example, for the following tasks, there is no design, or code, or test, or implementation:

- How much data can we move through a T1 line in the timeframe the processing window allows?
- Can our optical character readers (OCR) interpret the invoices being produced by an outside vendor?
- Is governmental agency approval likely within the time constraints with which we are working?

Project Management Control Systems

Project management control systems are automated software packages that typically execute on a personal computer. These products also execute on workstations, minicomputers, and mainframe

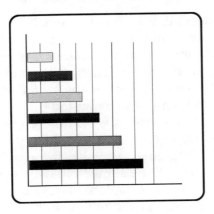

computers. Every IC uses these software packages to produce calendars for scheduling, histograms (vertical bars) and Gantt charts (horizontal bars) for timelines and budgets, and outlines for task prioritization. The calendars, graphical charts, and outlines these packages produce provide a medium for communication so people can look at the same thing and understand it the same way. These features in the project management software are excellent aids for the IC. However, these very same packages contain some features that you will have to decide for yourself whether they're appropriate for your implementation.

PERT and CPM

The Performance Evaluation and Review Technique (PERT) and the Critical Path Method (CPM) techniques of project management software have been excessively hyped and oversold. Many training organizations and software vendors would have you believe that once you've mastered these techniques of PERT and CPM you will be able to control most of the problems endemic to implementation management. The fact is that PERT/CPM and the other features of project management software are only a small element of the total implementation management apparatus. If you're looking for your project management software to solve or even alert you to all the implementation's problems, you could end up being very disappointed.

The PERT and CPM features of project management software

are tools for helping with resource allocation, resource leveling, and resolving scheduling conflicts. These tools were developed in the 1950s by engineers who were aware that task duration often can't be known with any practical certainty. With project management software you can lay out a PERT network of implementation tasks and identify their dependencies. Then the software will calculate which tasks and their dependencies require the longest time to accomplish. This is what is referred to as the "critical path." If any task on the "critical path" is late, then the entire implementation will be late. So the theory is that through the expenditure of resources (typically adding more people), you can shorten a task's duration and keep your implementation on time. Is this a valid assumption? If you're digging ditches you can certainly shorten task duration by adding more people. However, software development and implementation are exercises in complex human and technical relationships. What you find is that as you add more people in an attempt to shorten task duration you will invariably lengthen the time necessary to complete that task. What happens is that the people working on that task are distracted from their own work while they bring the new personnel up to speed on the myriad intricacies and details of the implementation; the net effect is to slow everything down.

> *Adding more people to a late project makes it later.*
>
> *—Brook's Law*

Figure 6.8 presents what's known as the Maximum Acceleration Factor. With productivity on one axis and people on the other the chart illustrates how adding more people may initially give the project a slight boost in productivity. However, the Maximum Acceleration Factor is quickly realized and the net effect of adding even more people actually slows the project down.

> *If a product is late with its implementation, I pull people off the project. If it's late again, I pull more people off.*
>
> *—Charles Wang*

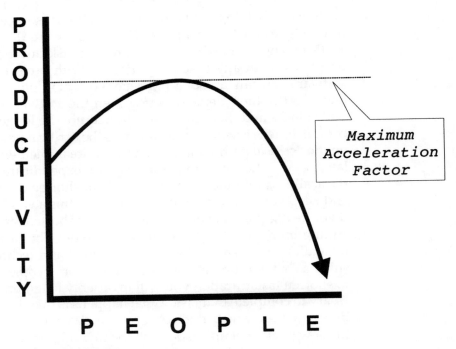

Figure 6.8.   Maximum Acceleration Factor

PERT charts can obscure the record of how time is actually spent, for a couple of reasons. First, ICs see numerous incidences where a minor technical problem becomes a major resource drain. And very often the technical problem isn't even listed as a task in the PERT chart. Second, it isn't politically expedient to re-estimate a task. Once a task has consumed its allotted time, any further work is hidden under some other task. No "slippage" in the implementation schedule is evident until most of the tasks have used their time allotments, which just so happens to coincide with the due date. The danger is that no time is left for corrective action.

PERT charts don't provide a good medium for communication. ICs have found implementation participants looking at them in JIP Implementation Planning Sessions and wondering "What is my part? Where do I fit in?" One implementation had a PERT chart that was 17 pages long! You certainly can't bring a chart that clunky into a JIP Session. Whose brain can get around a chart that big? So ICs usually condense the pertinent information down to some key elements that can be printed in a one-page document.

Project Management Software

You can't be an effective IC and spend all your time programming your project management software. Entering and updating all the data in the project management software can be a full-time job. Project management software is a tool, not a solution. ICs require the freedom to be inventive and flexible. They need tools that don't limit them. So on large implementations ICs budget for a technical specialist to program the project management software in the Implementation Resource Requirements. This frees the IC to coordinate the people issues. The IC needs to keep an ear to the ground, listening and looking for problems instead of focusing on a software package.

Metrics

Metrics are standards of measurement. For years, information systems pundits have been promoting the value of metrics. Metrics have value and can be utilized effectively when restructuring or stabilizing legacy systems. Metrics for legacy systems can be garnered by measuring the complexity and defects in the programming code. These metrics can then be used to determine the state of the system and help determine the time required to restructure it. However, the value of metrics for software development and implementation are circumspect. The pundits point to the housing industry, which has captured and codified standard measures of utility for construction. These kinds of measurements are practical for industries in which the products are mass-produced. However, information systems, and especially their implementations, are not mass-produced. The implementing of information systems doesn't just expand the business, it actually redefines it. The organizational structure of the company changes with each implementation. Since the implementation of a new system or product is unique, it's difficult (if not impossible) to measure and codify it before completion. ICs are usually wary of utilizing metrics when implementing a new system or product.

Groupware

"Groupware" is software that automates many of the logistical chores of the IC. While some of these logistical functions (like e-mail) have been around on mainframes for years, groupware is proliferating on desktop computers with graphical-user-interfaces (GUIs) that make them infinitely easier to use than their typically hostile mainframe predecessors.

The hierarchical organizational structure of yesteryear as illustrated in Figure 6.9 was not conducive to the free flow of information. In fact, it was unidirectional in its flow of information. However, the network organizational structure of today, as illustrated in Figure 6.10, is conducive to the free flow of information. Groupware really exemplifies the network organizational structure. With groupware the flow of information is multi-directional and the lines of communication are much shorter. These short lines of communication are a prerequisite for implementation control and they can be coordinated by the IC through a groupware package. Every implementation is a network of *recombinant teams* (forming, breaking up, reforming). The actions and consequences of these recombinant teams can be orchestrated and monitored by the IC with groupware.

Groupware is revolutionizing the ways in which an IC coordinates an implementation. ICs can now perform many logistical tasks from their desktop instead of running around and trying to contact

Hierarchical Organization

INFORMATION FLOW

Figure 6.9.   **Hierarchical Organization Information Flow**

Network Organization

Figure 6.10.   Network Organization Information Flow

everyone personally. These packages have group appointment tools so the IC can view people's schedules to determine the best time for setting up a JIP Session. Since everyone is usually busy, the IC can send electronic JIP Session announcements that say, "I've determined that this time is mutually inconvenient for everyone, so please be there." These packages can monitor the e-mail you send and tell you which people intend to make the JIP Session, who will not attend, and who *hasn't even read* your e-mail announcement. Now the IC can maximize her time by making other arrangements with those people who said they can't attend, and then "working on" only those people who either refuse to attend or are ignoring her. The group appointment tools also enable the IC to schedule resources such as conference rooms, overhead projectors, and so forth.

With groupware packages the IC can easily build distribution lists that route her e-mail only to select groups of people. With distribution lists the IC doesn't have to enter the same set of IDs every day. ICs can use groupware packages to expedite implementation management by assigning tasks to the responsible person and tracking whether that task has been completed. If that person doesn't finish the assigned task, it stays on the Task Log and is visible on the desktop interface every day.

The Implementation Workbook can be built with the word processors, spreadsheets, graphics programs, project management packages, and groupware available on the desktop computer. For example, you can build a very complete Contact List using the groupware's address-book capability. The Implementation Workbook can reside on a server so that everyone on the network can peruse it at their discretion. Obviously, only the IC should have update privileges. It's still a good idea to print the Implementation Workbook and maintain the hardcopy in a loose-leaf binder, adding and replacing pages as necessary to keep it updated. You'll find the hardcopy handy when you have to run a meeting without a wireless network for accessing the server from your portable computer.

CONCLUSION

If there is one thing people hate in the information systems industry, it's *more forms*! This chapter is not intended to burden the IC with more forms, or sound like those top-heavy methodologies that serve more to waste trees than assist the implementation process. As an IC you should tailor the Implementation Plan I've presented so that it will work for *your* particular implementation. You may need to add additional items to your Implementation Plan, because the components of the plan detailed in this chapter are by no means exhaustive. The size of your implementation will dictate what you find necessary to add, and how much to use of the Implementation Plan described herein. For large implementations you will need a complete and comprehensive Implementation Plan. For small implementations a scaled-down variation will suffice. Just remember that as the IC you are responsible for coordinating all aspects of the implementation, and the quality of your Implementation Plan goes a long way toward determining the quality of your implementation.

CHAPTER 7

Testing the Implementation: Validating Assumptions

Testing seeks to find errors of commission and omission made during a system's or product's design, development, and (ultimately) implementation. It's hard to conceive of the possibility that you could test too much. Obviously, you don't want to miss an implementation date, but the fact remains that the more testing you do, the higher the probability that your implementation will run smoothly. Testing can remedy erroneous assumptions, ill-conceived designs, and programming efforts that have been hurried due to resource or time constraints. Testing is an implementation's last line of defense.

The computer industry in general and information systems in particular have gotten bad names from rushing systems and products to implementation without adequate testing. Hurrying the testing effort is also why it's so difficult to instill the concept of quality in the developers, and to install quality in the delivered systems and products.

TEST EVERYTHING!

You must test everything that you built into your Implementation Plan at the JIP Implementation Planning Sessions. When ICs say, "Test everything," they're not referring so much to the testing of every conditional in every computer program as they are to every item in the Implementation Plan.

Once upon an implementation, a data center was moving from one location to a new one on the other side of town. Some of the items in the IC's Implementation Plan dealt with street parking on the entire side of the block next to the data centers that would allow the trucks to get in and out of the alleys, and with elevators for moving the mainframe computers up and down the floors, and with security clearance for the teamsters so that they could go in and out of the data centers. To test her Implementation Plan, the IC coordinated with the police department to make sure the alleys would be posted and that any cars parked in violation of the posting would be towed away the night of the implementation. She also physically inspected the elevators to make sure they were big enough, and could carry the weight of the mainframe computers. She also checked with the security force at the data centers to make sure the teamsters would be allowed into the data centers to perform the move. All this is part of testing.

ICs have screwed up more implementations by failing to test every item on their Implementation Plan than they have by failing to test the software to be implemented. This particular IC was sensitive to this fact because she had previously "blown" a new-product demonstration for another organization. This happened because the teamsters could not fit the mini-computer into the elevator the morning of the presentation. She ultimately got a crane to lift the mini-computer up the outside of the building, but the demonstration was delayed a day and her Project Manager was not happy.

Testing Assumptions

ICs know that you must verify your assumptions by validating what really works and what doesn't. ICs are continually amazed at how business users and even technical specialists will make assumptions that seem so reasonable and self-evident that no one bothers to verify or even question the supposition upon which the assumption is based. ICs try to substantiate every assumption by testing or modeling with real-world data.

The first assumption you make will impede your implementation.

—IC's truism

Once upon an implementation, the IC had a business user who said, "If you debit all the customer accounts by this much, the company will net this much in interest." The IC enlisted the help of several programmers, who modeled a scenario that enabled them to run simulations of posting debits to the accounts. Then they determined how many accounts had actually shown an interest-bearing difference The business-user's assumption was proven to be valid. By taking the time to prove this assumption, the IC strengthened the business case for enlisting and building support for the implementation.

Iterative Testing

If a project hasn't used the Joint Application Development (JAD) Workshop for defining requirements and developing specifications, that project will probably be trying to implement an unstable system or product. The only way to bring stability to the system to be implemented is to iteratively test it. Wanting to test the system repeatedly can prove to be a real problem for ICs dealing with business users who are dilettantes insofar as information systems are concerned.

Once upon an implementation, the system was developed from a particularly poor specification document. The IC put the question to the business user, "I believe we should iterate throughout the testing. How many iterations do you think we should perform?" To which the business user responded, "Well, probably three or four." The IC tactfully told the business user that it could very well take 25 to 30 iterations of testing to ensure a satisfactory level of correctness and reliability within the new system to be implemented. Fortunately, this IC was able to successfully educate the business user about the realities of information systems development and implementation, and thereby persuaded the business user to perform enough iterations of the testing so as to guarantee an operative system.

Cycling-Through

For every testing effort the number of logical (vs. physical) days to "cycle-through" must be determined. Typically you will need to

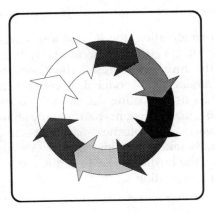

cycle-through at every day-end, week-end, month-end, quarter-end, and year-end. How many more-or-less logical days to cycle-through is uniquely specific to the system or product you're implementing. How long it will take to cycle-through each application must also be determined. Every systems group knows how long it takes them to cycle-through their particular application's test-kit. Bear in mind that applications could have large disparities in terms of the amount of time needed to cycle through one logical day. Some applications take a maximum of a few hours while others take a minimum of several days. After documenting how long it takes each application involved in the implementation to cycle-through one logical test-day, you can make some reasonable time projections of how long it will take to cycle one logical test-day through all the applications. Then you can start to develop a test plan with reasonable time-frames for each iteration of a cycle.

ICs find that it's always a good idea to check with the personnel on site to determine from their experience how long it usually takes their test-kit to cycle-through an entire day. Someone will tell you at the coffee machine, "Believe me, it will take four days for the test to cycle an entire day through our test-kit. It may go faster, but I have yet to see it." That will give you a benchmark for that application's test cycle.

It can take up to a week to test one logical day for several reasons. First, there are always limited test resources, which your implementation is competing for with other groups. Second, there are invariably some operational problems, such as the technology group adding hardware or upgrading some portion of the operating system software. Third, there are the logistical realities. Application Group A (AGA) stays late and guts it out to finish their testing at 10 P.M. But Application Group B (AGB), who's next in line for the test files, doesn't show up until 10 A.M. the next day. Then when AGB is ready to hand off the test files to the next group in line, Application Group C (AGC) is out for a long lunch because someone is leaving their department. It goes on and on like this, and it's an IC's typical nightmare.

JIP Test Planning Sessions

The implementation test plan is developed in the JIP Test Planning Sessions. Anyone and everyone who has a part, or is impacted by the system or product to be implemented, participates in the JIP Test Planning Sessions. In the JIP Test Planning Sessions and smaller working sessions the generalities and specifics of the implementation test plan are defined, developed, and documented.

JIP Test Planning:

1. Identify who are the *players*.
2. Designate for each area the *key test person*.
3. Identify who will *sign off* the testing.
4. Establish the *criteria* that drive the testing.
5. *Schedule* the testing cycles.
6. Identify to whom the *reports will be issued*.
7. Define the *testing terminology*.

The Players

The first thing to be done in every JIP Test Planning Session is to identify who are the players (the systems, the groups, and the people) involved in the implementation testing effort. This becomes the organizational infrastructure for the implementation testing effort. Obviously, the players involved in the implementation testing effort may have been identified in a JIP Preplanning Session. However, it's always a good idea to revisit this issue at the beginning of the full-blown JIP Test Planning Session to make sure that no one or no group has been overlooked.

Key Test Persons

Each system, group, division, or whatever must designate, or at least agree upon, one person who will be the single source of integrated responsibility for their area's testing effort.

Sign Off

The JIP Test Planning Session should identify those persons who will sign off the various types of tests. As detailed later in this chapter, there are many different types of testing. Therefore, the person responsible for signing off each of these types of testing needs to be identified.

Establishing Criteria

The IC should meet with each of the persons responsible for signing off each type of testing and determine their criteria for signing off. Establishing their standards for acceptance is important because these criteria will effectively drive the implementation testing schedule. For example, do the implementation testers need to test with production data? If so, what *kind* of testing with production data does the signer expect? How *much* testing with production data does the signer expect? How *many* cycles do the implementation testers need to go through to make sure the signer's concerns are addressed? Establishing criteria like these is crucial because if even one person refuses to sign off some part of the implementation testing, then the product or system can't be implemented.

Developing the Test Schedule

Once the criteria are established, the implementation testing schedule can be developed. When you know what the signers expect, the implementation testers can guesstimate how long the various types of testing should take. This is an imperfect science but at least you'll be operating from some sort of baseline when producing the testing schedule. Figure 7.1 is an example of an Implementation Test Schedule.

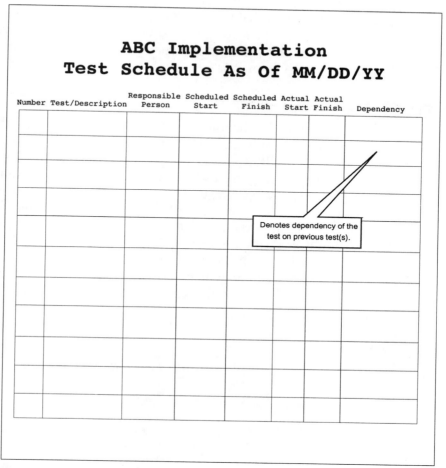

Figure 7.1.   Implementation Test Schedule

Issuing Reports

JIP Test Planning Sessions should identify to whom the various testing reports will be issued. The principal reports are the problem reports and the change request reports. The protocol for resolving items on these reports must also be established in the JIP Session. For example, it may be decided that problem reports should be kept within the application group unless the item in question impacts a downstream application. The IC really doesn't want to see every problem report on an application group's programming problems.

Of course, if that application group is three weeks behind schedule you might have to get involved in their problem reporting. The problem reports and the change request reports are described in detail in Chapter 8.

Terminology Used in Testing

Everybody in the information systems industry has their own ideas about what the different terms used in testing mean. Therefore, defining, codifying, and documenting the terminology that is employed during the testing is crucial to the implementation's success. Otherwise everyone will be using different words to mean the same type of testing. For example, what one person refers to as "unit testing," another person calls "modular testing," and yet another person calls "program testing."

The IC leads the discussion that gets consensus on what the testing terminology will be for this particular implementation. The Scribe writes the definitions of the terms on the Session Boards. Fig-

Testing Terms and Definitions

Type of Testing	Definition	Synonyms
Unit Testing	each individual software unit	modular or program
System Testing	every program within a particular system	application
Interface Testing	interface between two systems	handoff or handshake
Integration Testing	an entire 'stream' of systems	all applications
User Acceptance Testing	an entire 'stream' of systems	UAT
Regression Testing	pre-existing functionality not impacted by the implementation	retrogression
Stress Testing	doing 'bad things' to the systems	non-sensible
Volume Testing	full production volumes of data	capacity
Restart Testing	systems can be restarted as required	rerun

Figure 7.2.   Testing Terms and Definitions Chart

ure 7.2 is an example of a Testing Terms and Definitions matrix drawn on the Session Boards. After the session the IC writes up and distributes the matrix. Everyone who receives a copy understands what these terms mean for this implementation. This matrix should be developed for every implementation, even if the same personnel from a previous implementation are involved in the current implementation. If the terminology isn't written down and made clear, the implementation participants can quickly get out-of-sorts with one another, and real communication and understanding will suffer.

Implementation Test Plan

The Implementation Test Plan is an English narration with descriptive graphical documentation. The IC should write a synopsis of the Implementation Test Plan that is brief, to the point, and comprehensible. If the test plan is too long and unwieldy, people will become frustrated and won't actively participate in the testing effort. They'll "go passive" and rationalize, "Oh, I'll wait until the application that calls mine tells me it's time to test."

Once upon an implementation, the organization documented their Implementation Test Plan in a chart that was too large to even publish, and what they did publish turned out to be unreadable. It consisted of cryptic codes and tasks enumerated on 12 sheets of paper. This document showed the schedule related to the testing cycles (logical day 1, logical day 2, and so forth), but no one could understand the interrelationships amongst the many application groups' testing efforts. To its dismay, the organization found that most people weren't going to crawl through the 12-page document when all they wanted to know was, "What is my part?" and "How do I impact others?" and "How can others impact me?"

Test Kits

A test kit is an "environment" that duplicates the functionality of the information system in production. This could include, but is certainly not limited to, the application code, the job control language (JCL), the online or GUI interface, the distributed systems protocol, the database management system (DBMS), the network data mover, the job scheduler, and so forth.

ICs find that test kits in large organizations tend to be mediocre. In some organizations the test kits are either inadequate or don't even exist. Programmers just grab production JCL, "kluge" it to execute those programs they're either adding or changing, and then test. This quick-and-dirty attitude toward testing causes real nightmares for ICs because they want to conduct all the implementation testing in a systematic manner. ICs can't always dissuade people from testing in a haphazard manner if that is what they are used to, because entrenched work habits are very difficult to change.

Test-Beds

A test-bed refers to data that each information systems group uses for testing their particular application's functionality. The test-bed data is usually permanent and not to be altered unless explicitly directed by management. The organization may also have a separate test-bed of data for system-wide integrated testing efforts.

Test Cases

A test case is a scenario that provides an outline for testing a particular function or functions of the new system or product to be implemented. Test cases are generated in JIP Test Case Development Sessions. It's very easy to perform an inordinate amount of testing and yet never execute major areas of the application code to be implemented. Therefore, test cases must be developed with much forethought to make certain that every function—whether added, changed, or impacted—is tested. How many test cases are needed to test the system or product to be implemented is decided in the JIP Test Case Development Session. Figure 7.3 is an example of a Test Case Chart drawn on the Session Boards. These test cases are the basis for the development of the test scripts.

Test Scripts

A test script is a combination of procedures that must be enacted and data that must be acted upon to test a particular function of the new system or product to be implemented. The test scripts are developed from the test cases generated in the JIP Test Case Development Sessions. To really ensure the validity of the testing, it's best if you don't allow the test scripts to be developed by the program-

Test Case Chart

Business Event	System/Application	Database(s)	Output	Test Script Developer
service request	Service Order Entry	SOEDB	service order	SOE Group
billing inquiry	Service Order Billing	SOBDB	transaction audit log	SOB Group

Figure 7.3. **Test Case Chart**

mers who are coding the new system. If the programmers who code the programs also develop the test scripts, you're in effect asking them to police themselves. This is not a good idea if you want to implement a quality system. Obviously, you still need the programmer's input to develop comprehensive test cases. You can get this input at a JIP Test Case Development Session, and then make someone else responsible for doing further research and writing up the test scripts.

Who Develops the Test Cases?

The application group that is the principal participant in the development of the test cases, and in effect is driving the implementation testing effort, is the group for whom *the testing will be the most difficult*. The rationale behind this is that the testing effort will be greatly expedited if every application group supports the work of whichever group has the hardest job of testing.

> *Who drives the testing effort?*
> *The group whose application is the most immutable, the most limiting, and therefore the most difficult to drive.*
>
> —*IC Truism*

Once upon an implementation, the senior manager insisted that the "darling" of the information systems groups, which was the graphical-user interface group named "We're The GUI Darlings (WGD)," drive all the implementation testing by being the principal participant in the development of every test case. The senior manager did this because the corporation had invested the most money in the WGD group, so to the senior manager's way of thinking, WGD was the most important. However, from a testing point of view, the WGD functionality was pure vanilla, especially when compared to the batch functions required of the application groups. The batch functions were bearing the brunt of the functionality being implemented for the new system and should have driven the testing effort. Unfortunately, every systems group had to use test scripts developed from the WGD group's test cases, which meant that many batch functions were not thoroughly tested in integration with the other applications. Needless to say, there were some major problems when the new system went "live."

Massaging Test Data

Manipulating test data to make it conform to parameters required to test the new system or product to be implemented is an ugly process. Changing the data in the test-bed, either by hand or with quick-and-dirty programming, is sure to introduce additional problems and will definitely compromise the validity and reliability of the test-bed. However, many times there is no other way. Just be forewarned, and lookout for problems and inconsistencies in the test-bed.

JIP Test-Kit Synchronization Sessions

JIP Test-Kit Synchronization Sessions are forums in which the application groups try to get their test kits in synch for the implementation testing effort. The robustness of each application group's test kit and the cohesion between the test kits looms as a large issue for a multiple-application implementation. To ensure any reliability, correctness, and quality in the implementation, you must do thorough testing with every application group in concert.

The first thing to do in a JIP Test-Kit Synchronization Session is get all the test kits on the same calendar date. Then dates must be picked so that you're sure the testing hits the weekly, monthly, quarterly, and year-end cycles. Remember that adjusting for leap year and even century may also be issues. Getting all the dates in the test kits in synch and picking dates to test usually involves a lot of work and can take numerous JIP Sessions.

Once upon an implementation, the IC had a number of especially tough JIP Test-Kit Synchronization Sessions that synchronized two organization's test kits in support of a merger of their information systems after one company bought the other. The dates in the test kits were 10 years apart! To get the test kits in synch, one organization had to change every date in its test-bed. Not only was this a mammoth undertaking but the reliability and credibility of the test-bed was jeopardized. When you start manipulating the data in the test-bed, its integrity becomes compromised. These were not the only problems with the synchronization process. By changing the dates in the test-bed, certain functions that were automatically tested by the old dates did not get executed with the new dates. So test-cases and scripts had to be developed to test those functions that people had for years taken for granted would be tested with any iteration of the test-kit.

Testing with Production Data

In terms of the correctness and reliability of the implemented system, there is no substitute for production data when testing. Test-kit data is usually frozen in time and therefore never reflects the current state of the production environment. Needless to say, there are security issues concerning production data but these can usually be resolved with encryption routines. Many times ICs identify major issues that were unknown because the organization hadn't been testing with production data.

A classic example of the usefulness of production data occurred when a programmer informed the IC facilitating the implementation effort that two of the thirty input files for the new system did not conform to the business-rules edits. Therefore, if the system was implemented as it was, every transaction on those two files would be rejected. The programmer only ascertained this fact because she started testing the system with the production files.

Volume Testing

Volume testing refers to testing the system or product to be implemented with the amount of data or number of transactions you can reasonably expect the system to encounter at its peak periods in the production environment. Volume testing resolves the capacity planning issues for the system to be implemented, such as, how long will a batch cycle take or how fast will an online system respond to a request at peak periods? The only way to make sure the system to be implemented will cycle or respond in the time frames promised is to perform volume testing.

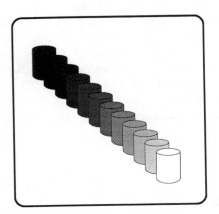

Murphy's Second Law: Everything takes longer than you think.

The second issue that volume testing resolves is that every function in fact gets tested and every glitch found. Test-beds are usually small, so a major effort is needed to create records that approximate everything that could possibly happen in the production environment. This can take time. However, this process can be facilitated with volume testing because every information system ever built already contains many internal controls, such as reject reports, exception reports, debit/credit balancing reports, and so forth. By pumping volumes of records or transactions through the test-kits you can easily see what fails or falls out on the system's reports.

Once upon an implementation, the job involved the merger of the information systems of two large organizations. The merger was so large that the distribution centers across the country could not all be converted at the same time. The tricky part of the conversion process was in maintaining the "linkages" between the accounts. If a customer had an account at Distribution Center A (DCA) and another account at Distribution Center B (DCB), and DCA was converted when DCB wasn't, then the information systems had to be able to track those "linkages" between the accounts in DCA and DCB even though the accounts no longer looked similar due to the conversion. It would take a team of statisticians to extrapolate all the possibilities to determine how many "linkages" needed to be tested to statistically guarantee that all the "linkage" probabilities had been covered.

The IC was able to sell senior management on the strategy that in addition to testing with the test-beds and generated test scripts, they should also perform volume testing with the production databases. With the IC's assistance, senior management realized that no one could possibly envision every "linkage" situation that might occur and then build the appropriate test case to simulate that scenario. With volume testing, the conversion had a much better shot at testing all the "linkage" possibilities.

Some people believe that the volume of test data is determined by how many test cases are developed into test scripts. Other people just don't see the point of pumping volumes of data through the test-kits after a considerable effort has been made to prove all the new system's functionality with generated test scripts. While testing with test scripts and the resident test-beds is an important component of the entire testing process, the importance of volume testing cannot be minimized.

GUI Testing

The Graphical-User Interface (GUI) is replacing the character-based interface for the business user. Testing a character-based interface is fairly straightforward because the business user only has a limited number of options. However, with the GUI interface the business user's options are immense, so the testing is much more difficult. The testing effort must push all the wrong buttons, select all the wrong icons, and disobey the standard operating procedures to make sure the GUI interface can respond to such abuse intelligently and not get hung-up.

Implementation Testing

The entire implementation testing effort can be subdivided into two major components: the application group's testing responsibilities and the IC's testing responsibilities. While the application groups test to ensure the correctness of their information systems, the IC coordinates the testing amongst all the application and technology groups to ensure the organization-wide operability of the new system or product being implemented.

Application Group's Testing Responsibilities

Since the application groups test their own application, that testing responsibility is typically beyond the IC's domain. However, a brief description of the types of testing the application groups should perform is provided here so you can at least check on each group and make sure they are in fact doing the appropriate testing. If they aren't, then that becomes an implementation issue and, as such, it does come under the IC's domain. Figure 7.4 is an example of a Test Plan Chart drawn on the Session Boards for the application group's testing.

Application Group's Testing Responsibilities

- Unit Test
- System Test
- Stress Test
- Parallel Test

Test Plan Chart
For The Application Groups

Test	Scope	Verifies	Test Data	Person(s) Responsible	Sign-Off
Unit Test	each program	programs	test-bed	programmer	team lead
System Test	system	application	test-bed	system team	system manager
Stress Test	everything	robustness	bad input	system teams	team leaders
Parallel Test	system	new vs. old	test-bed	system teams	team leaders
Regression Test	as required	pre-existing functionality	regression test-bed	system teams	team leaders
Rerun Test	system	system restart	test-bed	system teams	system manager

Figure 7.4.   **Test Plan Chart for the Application Groups**

- Regression Test
- ReStart/ReRun Test

In *Unit* testing, the programmers test the programs they have either written or changed to make sure that the module conforms to the specifications they were given.

In *Systems* testing, every program in the application is tested in concert to make sure the application as an integrated whole conforms to the specification document.

In *Stress* testing, the programmers do horrible things to the application, especially its human interfaces, to make sure the application will respond in a logical way.

In *Parallel* testing, a new application is tested against an existing application (or portions thereof) by using the same data for both tests, to make sure that the new application will process data in the same way as the old application. Parallel testing isn't always applicable because the application to be implemented may be totally new to the organization.

In *Regression* testing, the functions not changed in the application code are tested to make sure their functionality has not been impacted by the implementation's programming changes.

In *Restart/Rerun* testing, the application is abnormally terminated or brought down during processing, and then restarted or rerun to make sure that no transactions have been lost or that no data has been corrupted.

IC's Testing Responsibilities

The IC is responsible for all testing amongst the application and technology groups. The IC coordinates the organization-wide "joint" test effort of every group and person involved in the implementation. The IC makes sure that every aspect of the system or product to be implemented is tested from start to finish. Figure 7.5 is an example of a Test Plan Chart for the Joint Implementation Testing drawn on the Session Boards.

IC's Testing Responsibilities

- Joint Integration Test
- Joint User Acceptance Test
- Joint Dry-Run Test

Joint Integration Testing

In Joint Integration Testing, every application and technology participating in the implementation are tested in concert with one another

Test Plan Chart
For The Joint Implementation Testing

Test	Scope	Verifies	Person Responsible	Sign-Off
Joint Integration Testing	every system & application	every interface	IC	system managers
Joint User Acceptance Testing	every system & application	implementation OK'd by the business partner	IC	business partners
Joint Dry-Run Testing	every system & application	organization wide systems execution	IC	senior manager(s)

Figure 7.5.   **Test Plan Chart for the Joint Implementation Testing**

to guarantee the organization-wide operability and correctness of the new system or product. Joint Integration Testing is always the hardest part of the System Development Life Cycle. Despite this fact, most project plans allot 90 percent of the time for design, code, and unit testing. This leaves only 10 percent of the time for Joint Integration Testing, which can cause a lot of frustration.

How come the first 90 percent of the project plan took six months and the last 10 percent took six months?

—IS Industry Lament

Machinery tends to break at the moving part, and information systems likewise tend to fail at the point at which they integrate. Problems within an application can usually be corrected quite easily. But if one application gives another application a wrong length record or a message it wasn't prepared to receive, then you've got major problems. With all the miscommunication you can have within a small group, imagine how much miscommunication you can have across several and especially many groups. The integration complexities increase dramatically as more applications and technologies need to be coordinated within the Joint Integration Testing effort.

Once upon an implementation, the Joint Integration Testing was performed for the daily and weekly cycles only. The monthly, quarterly, and yearly-cycle testing was left to each application group. This proved to be a real disaster, although this didn't become evident until those cycles occurred in production. Ironically, under Post-Implementation Review, each application group was able to prove that its portion of the new system had been fully tested and performed correctly for the monthly, quarterly, and yearly cycles. However, the new system didn't work right because there were data-handling discrepancies among the individual applications on these cycles. The Joint Integration Testing had not gone far enough to prove that the new system functioned correctly as an integrated whole on the monthly, quarterly, and yearly cycles.

ICs understand that during Joint Integration Testing it is important not to go on to the next application's testing until the preceding application's test is verified and correct. Therefore, it can sometimes take five calendar days to test just one logical day. When a logical day is proven correct, then the joint integration testing can proceed with the next logical day. Typically ICs test six to nine cycles or logical days. They want to hit the daily, weekly, monthly, quarterly, and yearly cycles. The idea is to test the organization's most complex processing days.

Joint User-Acceptance Testing

Joint User-Acceptance Testing is done after you have completed all the cycles for the Joint Integration Test. Then you start the entire Joint Integration Test process again for the business-user's acceptance. If you have "gutted it out" in the Joint Integration Testing and resolved all the problems, the Joint User-Acceptance Testing should go a lot faster and smoother. The test output will definitely be much cleaner, and the business users will look at it and say, "Yep, that's what I needed to see."

Joint Dry-Run Testing

Joint Dry-Run Testing is a trial execution of the organization-wide information systems with full volume production databases. Joint Dry-Run Testing is for large implementations that impact the information systems of the organization enterprise-wide. Joint Dry-Run Testing is usually conducted over a weekend with both the new systems and new hardware. The organization may balk at the time and resources required to perform a comprehensive Joint Dry-Run Test. However, for a really large implementation, anything less will impact the implemented system's operational reliability.

Optimists vs. Pessimists

Everyone is familiar with the aphorism that optimists see the glass as half full while pessimists see it as half empty. It can be tough to determine who has the better perception of the implementation testing. It's possible for the implementation testing effort to be overwhelmed by nit-pickers or under-supported by those in a hurry.

Figure 7.6.   **Communicate/Validate Wheel**

The IC must make the "judgment call" about which perception is most valid and then support that view. The best way of determining which perception to support is: communicate, communicate, communicate, and then validate. Figure 7.6 is a symbolic representation of that scenario.

CHAPTER 8

Implementing the System: Logistics of the Implementation

The logistical problems of implementing a system or product are administered by several Implementation Management Teams. The duties of these teams, the names of the people who compose them, and everyone's roles and responsibilities on these teams are documented in the Implementation Plan. The Implementation Plan also outlines what tools the Implementation Management Teams will use.

The Implementation Management Teams are made up of managers who are participants in the implementation effort. As implementation participants these managers will be reviewing and signing off various aspects of the Implementation Plan, so they should be well aware of their roles and responsibilities in the Implementation Management Teams. Since the extent of their participation is documented in the Implementation Plan, these managers have ample opportunity, if they so desire, to present business reasons why they shouldn't participate in one or more of the Implementation Management Teams.

How often the Implementation Management Teams meet is determined by the number or severity of logistical problems encountered. When, where—and even if—the Implementation Management Teams meet, is determined on a day-to-day basis. Figure 8.1 is a symbolic representation of the execution and coordination that must be exercised for an implementation to be successful.

Figure 8.1.   **Execution/Coordination Wheel**

IMPLEMENTATION MANAGEMENT TEAMS

Implementation Management Teams are designated and then published in the Implementation Plan to address specific problems that may arise during the new system or product's implementation. Some of these teams may never actually assemble or deploy because the problems the team was assigned to address might never occur. Since ICs typically have little or no authority within an organization, they cannot command anyone to serve, but they are free to negotiate, connive, or beg those persons they prefer to become members of the team.

Implementation Management Teams Are Populated By:

- Volunteers.
- Persons whose area of responsibility makes their participation obvious.

- Persons requested by the IC because of their expertise and insight.
- The IC.

The IC should contact every person on each team and confirm with them or inform them about what their role will be on the particular team. It's conceivable that someone could be on several teams. By contacting each team member personally, the IC seeks to obtain their commitment and support for the team's responsibilities. Then when problems arise at three o'clock in the morning they won't be as angry about receiving your phone call.

The Implementation Management Teams are populated by all different levels of management, depending on the problems to be addressed. The managers from the higher levels of the organization are the ones who have the authority to solve problems in their areas of responsibility. Other managers who are good to have on a team are those who know (or at least understand) what would be best for a particular information system or systems.

Types of Implementation Management Teams

- Installation Management
- Problem Report
- Problem Management
- Change Management

Installation Management Team

The Installation Management Team deals with problems that occur as the system or product is actually being installed in the production environment. This team's responsibility is obviously "mission-critical," and its members should not be out of town on the night of the installation. However, if the installation proceeds without flaw, they may not even be called. Having an Installation Management Team ready to deal with any problems is essential; if needed, the availability of this team will save a tremendous amount of time. When you have a problem in the wee hours of the morning on installation day, you won't have to scurry around trying to determine which people should be involved in the problem-solving process, what roles they should play, and how you can get in contact with them.

The Installation Management Team Is Comprised Of:

1. The senior manager responsible for an area of information systems.
2. Those mid-level managers responsible for the particular information systems in that area.
3. The IC and anyone else the IC asks to attend.

ICs have been known to "blow" installations simply because they didn't have an Installation Management Team ready when problems occurred. If these ICs had had a team ready, the problems in most cases could have been quickly rectified. With no Installation Management Team available, these otherwise rectifiable problems dragged on for hours, and in some cases, for days.

If and when an installation problem occurs, the IC first speaks with all the knowledgeable participants about the problem. Then the IC outlines to the Installation Management Team what the problem is and the reasoning behind everyone's opinions, which may be conflicting. After the team deliberates and discusses the problem—and only then—should the IC ask, "Well, what is to be done?" The Installation Management Team will determine a solution, and identify who is responsible for and who is assigned to fix the problem.

Problem Report Team

The Problem Report Team reviews Problem Reports as they occur during testing. If there isn't a process for establishing where problems should reside, it's easy to lose *days* stumbling around trying to determine who should be involved, and when and where these people should be assembled to work on the problem. If there's a Problem Report Team, precious time isn't lost trying to get a problem identified, reviewed, prioritized, and assigned to the right hands. ICs always try to get the implementation's "key" managers to participate on this team. If there are numerous application groups involved in the implementation then just a few managers should participate on the Problem Report Team. You don't want the team to be over-populated, which would impair its ability to quickly resolve problems.

The Problem Report Team Is Comprised Of:

1. Those managers responsible for the application groups doing the implementation testing.
2. The IC and anyone else the IC asks to attend.

When debating whether to report a problem, remember that in the information systems industry, <u>one of anything is a trend</u>.

—IC truism

A form for Problem Reports is published in the Implementation Test Plan. The IC should let everyone know about any and all circumstances that require reports to be filled out, and inform them that all reports are to be delivered to the IC. Problems that are localized within an application group and can be resolved with that group's own expertise do not require Problem Reports. The Problem Report Team and the IC are only interested in problems that cut across application groups and/or impact other systems, whether inside or outside the organization.

A common scenario for a Problem Report occurs when a downstream application group identifies a problem. They write a Problem Report stating that the test case didn't respond the way it was supposed to, and then go on to say that it isn't their problem. Their report will say, "The upstream application gave us a bad transaction." But the upstream application group will swear that the transaction was valid when they shipped it downstream. Without a Problem Report Team the problem will become orphaned and lay around for days while the application groups pass the buck. The Problem Report and a Problem Report Team provide a process for resolving the issue so that valuable time isn't lost.

Problem Management Team

When a problem that was routed to its assigned area of responsibility by the Problem Report Team hasn't been resolved in a day or two, the IC calls in the Problem Management Team for that area to effect a solution. Typically, there are various Problem Management Teams to address different areas of the implementation. The IC must make sure that a representative from every part of the implementation effort participates in at least one Problem Management Team. Early on, the IC lets these people know to which Problem Management Team(s) they belong. Problem Reports always need to be addressed quickly, so if and when they start to arrive, the Problem Management Team people have been identified, know their roles, and know the teams in which they will participate. Problem Management Teams are planned for and documented in the Implementation Plan. Then if there's a problem, the responsible people can immediately sit down and talk about the problem with the right data in their hands—which greatly expedites the problem-resolution process.

Problem Management Teams Are Comprised Of:

1. Those managers responsible for a specific area (such as an information system, an application programming group, and so forth).
2. The IC and anyone else the IC asks to attend.

Once upon an implementation, the whole effort came to an impasse. Entire nodes on the network ground to a halt and hundreds of people were unable to do their work. The IC had to hustle around to organize those people with the expertise and application knowledge to address the problem area. The team the IC assembled then looked at the technology and systems, and finally determined what the problems were. Although the team was able to resolve the problems in the end, there was a tremendous gap between the time that the IC decided to assemble a team and the time it started producing results. It was a disaster, particularly in terms of the confidence lost in the implementation by the business users in the field. They had been thrashed. The IC belatedly realized that there should have been a Problem Management Team in place before the problems arose.

Change Management Team

The Change Management Team reviews all items necessitating programming changes. The most common issues for the Change Management Team are mismatched expectations. For example, there is a mismatched expectation when someone realizes, "Hey, this requirement wasn't fleshed out," or "Oops, what she construed to be a balancing report isn't what I had in mind." With the IC as the facilitator, the business user and the manager(s) responsible for the programming can negotiate a workable solution for any changes.

The Change Management Team brings stability and credibility to the implementation effort by not letting "hot-shot" programmers make undocumented changes to the programming code. By forming a Change Management Team the IC ensures that any and every change is negotiated between the business users and the programming managers, and then documented for Configuration Management.

The Change Management Team Is Comprised Of:

1. The business user of the system or product being implemented.
2. The manager(s) responsible for the application group(s) doing the programming (where the most serious change-management issues are going to occur).
3. The IC and anyone else the IC asks to attend.

Implementation Management Team Tools

There are various tools the Implementation Management Teams employ to do their work. These tools provide the members of the team with the necessary data they need to make their decisions. Some tools are described below, but the list isn't inclusive and shouldn't preclude you from creating and adding tools you feel are appropriate for your own implementation. Whatever tools you choose should be described in the Implementation Plan, including samples of their formats. This will guarantee uniformity among all the teams.

Types of Tools Used by Implementation Management Teams:

1. Problem Reports
2. Problem Log
3. Change Requests
4. Change Log
5. Configuration Management

Problem Reports. Problem Reports are forms for detailing everything that relates to a problem. Figure 8.2 is an example of a Problem Report.

Problem Log. The Problem Log is a document in which every Problem Report is recorded so that the IC can identify and track

```
┌─────────────────────────────────────────────────────────────────┐
│                                                                   │
│   ┌───────────────────────────────────────────────────────────┐  │
│   │  PROBLEM  REPORT          Page 1 of n  │
│   ├───────────────────────────────────┬───────────────────────┤  │
│   │ Implementation:                   │ Date Identified:      │  │
│   ├───────────────────────────────────┴───────────────────────┤  │
│   │ Originator:                                               │  │
│   ├───────────────────────────────────┬───────────────────────┤  │
│   │ Originator Phone Number:          │ E-Mail ID:            │  │
│   ├───────────────────────────────────┴───────────────────────┤  │
│   │ Problem Description:                                      │  │
│   │                                                           │  │
│   │                                                           │  │
│   ├───────────────────────────────────────────────────────────┤  │
│   │ Systems Impacted By The Problem:                          │  │
│   │                                                           │  │
│   ├───────────────────────────────────────────────────────────┤  │
│   │ Software Impacted In The Problem:                         │  │
│   │                                                           │  │
│   ├───────────────────────────────────────────────────────────┤  │
│   │ Hardware Impacted By The Problem:                         │  │
│   │                                                           │  │
│   ├───────────────────────────────────────────────────────────┤  │
│   │ Implementation Effort - The Problem's Impact:             │  │
│   │                                                           │  │
│   ├───────────────────────────────────────────────────────────┤  │
│   │ Organization's Systems - The Problem's Impact:            │  │
│   │                                                           │  │
│   ├───────────────────────────────────┬───────────────────────┤  │
│   │ Problem Logged By:                │ Date Logged:          │  │
│   └───────────────────────────────────┴───────────────────────┘  │
│                                                                   │
└─────────────────────────────────────────────────────────────────┘
```

Figure 8.2.   **Problem Report**

every problem to its resolution. The Problem Log also serves as a repository for information pertaining to coordinated problem-solving efforts. It's conceivable that the same problem could be reported several times under different circumstances and guises. Figure 8.3 is an example of a Problem Log.

Change Requests.   Change Requests are forms detailing everything pertaining to a requested change. Figure 8.4 is an example of a Change Request.

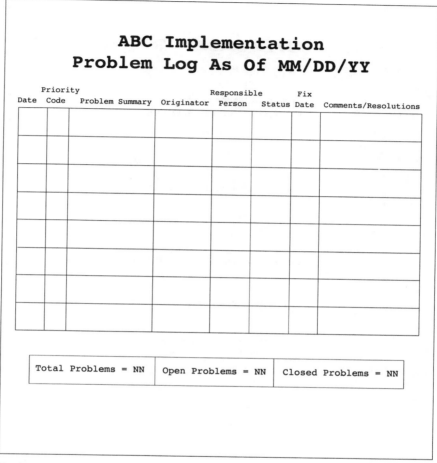

Figure 8.3.   Problem Log

Change Log.   The Change Log is a document in which every Change Request is recorded so the IC can identify and track every requested change and its ultimate resolution. The Change Log also serves as a repository for information pertaining to coordinated modification efforts. It's conceivable that additional changes could be piggybacked onto an initial change with minimal impact and expense. For example, if the programmers are already making one change to a program, it's likely they could make one or more additional changes at the same time. Figure 8.5 is an example of a Change Log.

```
┌──────────────────────────────────────────────────────────────┐
│                                                              │
│   CHANGE  REQUEST            Page 1 of n                     │
│  ┌──────────────────────────────┬─────────────────────────┐ │
│  │ Implementation:              │ Date Requested:         │ │
│  ├──────────────────────────────┴─────────────────────────┤ │
│  │ Requester:                                             │ │
│  ├──────────────────────────────┬─────────────────────────┤ │
│  │ Requester Phone Number:      │ E-Mail ID:              │ │
│  ├──────────────────────────────┴─────────────────────────┤ │
│  │ Description Of Requested Change:                       │ │
│  │                                                        │ │
│  ├────────────────────────────────────────────────────────┤ │
│  │ Business Reason That Supports The Change:              │ │
│  ├────────────────────────────────────────────────────────┤ │
│  │ Consequences Of NOT Making The Change:                 │ │
│  ├────────────────────────────────────────────────────────┤ │
│  │ Implementation Effort - The Change's Impact:           │ │
│  ├────────────────────────────────────────────────────────┤ │
│  │ Organization's Systems - The Change's Impact:          │ │
│  ├────────────────────────────┬───────────────────────────┤ │
│  │ Change Accepted ☐ Rejected ☐ │ CMT Authorization:      │ │
│  ├────────────────────────────┴───────────────────────────┤ │
│  │ Reason For Rejection:                                  │ │
│  ├──────────────────────────────┬─────────────────────────┤ │
│  │ Change Logged By:            │ Date Logged:            │ │
│  └──────────────────────────────┴─────────────────────────┘ │
│                                                              │
└──────────────────────────────────────────────────────────────┘
```

Figure 8.4.   Change Request

Configuration Management.   Configuration Management usually refers to automated software used to track every programming module being changed or written in support of the system or product to be implemented. Such packages can be stand-alone products that execute on a personal computer, or alternatively, a component of a sophisticated CASE (Computer Aided Software Engineering) tool that resides on a mainframe computer. Configuration Management software identifies and tracks every programming module so that, on projects with numerous developers, anyone can tell which is the current version of each module. Configuration Management

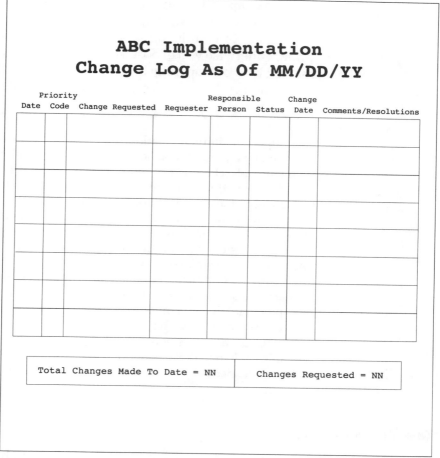

Figure 8.5.   Change Log

software can be invaluable for controlling the chaos within every implementation that is attributable to both the quantity of Change Requests submitted, and the fact that many of those changes are in the process of being made.

Conflicting Schedules

The IC should know the schedule of every other systems implementation or hardware installation in progress within the organization. Every organization has people—such as the strategic planning group or the capacity planning group—who are supposed to be planning these events. Although you might think they would address the issue of conflicting schedules, you can't make that assumption. Otherwise you expose yourself to the possibility of being whipsawed by a bureaucratic boondoggle in which the people and resources you need to be successful are not available.

> Once upon an implementation, the scheduled installation was preceded by a three-day holiday weekend. The senior-level management had scheduled a full-blown business-resumption test over this same three-day weekend for every information systems group within the organization. The issue for the IC was this: Were the system-group managers going to let their key personnel work on her implementation when they had their own mission-critical and highly visible business-resumption test to worry about? Not! Therefore, the business-resumption test would, in all probability, impact the IC's implementation. And if her implementation was delayed, the system-group managers could say, "We weren't able to implement your system on schedule because all our skilled resources were busy working on the business-resumption test." Because the IC was aware of this conflict long before it occurred, she was able to change the installation date and minimize the impact on her implementation.

Task Accountability

Task accountability seems straightforward enough. Tasks are defined, tasks are assigned, and then the tasks are tracked to completion. However, problems always occur when it comes to defining the boundaries of those tasks. Where my responsibility ends and yours begins is always a source of confusion. At "crunch time" it can also become a point of contention. "Crunch time" is the date when someone or some group is supposed to hand off their work (their deliverable) to another person or group. If that deliverable isn't exactly what the recipient group was expecting, the IC's got a dispute to resolve.

This issue of where responsibility begins and ends is always one of the biggest problems in human interaction. With implementations, the tasks (or parts thereof) that fall through the cracks between the beginning and end of responsibilities can have devastating conse-

Once upon another implementation, an application group within the organization—named GOOS (Got Our Own Schedule)—was so large it was a bureaucracy unto itself. GOOS had this timing formula it used for the phases of developing a new system. It would spend a third of the allotted time on analysis and specification, a third of the time on programming and unit testing, and a third of the time on integration testing. GOOS had separate groups within its bureaucracy for handling each one of these phases, and these groups passed off their work to one another. To make the IC's implementation date, the GOOS schedule specified that integration testing be performed in October. However, the IC needed them to perform her implementation's Joint Integration Testing in September—to ensure (in a timely manner) that the integration test data would go through all the other downstream applications.

Since GOOS was the most sought-after group for every implementation, it saw itself as the big dog on the block. When a group is used to being the "big dog," it doesn't like being the tail on the implementation. Or if it does become the tail on a particular implementation, it will try to wag the dog. The IC had a scheduling problem that was going to be difficult to negotiate. So she called and facilitated a JIP Test Planning Session at which all the other downstream applications presented their business cases for why they needed the GOOS group to get into integration testing earlier. If the IC had taken on the GOOS group alone, it would have been a very tough sell to convince GOOS to change its schedule. However, by resorting to the JIP Session and letting all the other applications present their specific reasons for needing the GOOS group to change its schedule, the IC was successful in getting the scheduling conflict resolved to the betterment of the implementation.

quences. ICs frequently have to deal with such situations. What you will find with every implementation is that people always tend to define their role as being smaller than anyone else would define it. Figure 8.6 is an illustration of this situation.

Therefore, the IC must *clearly define "hand-offs"* among organizations, groups, and individuals. All participants in the implementation must explicitly understand the deliverables they are responsible for handing off. For example, let's say someone is supposed to build

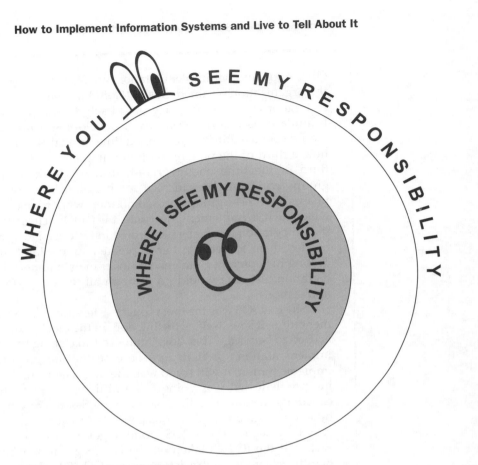

Figure 8.6. **Perceptions of Responsibility**

test scripts from the test cases developed in the JIP Test Case Development Session. If she delivers two scripts for each test case when the recipient of her work was expecting eight scripts for each test case, then you have a problem.

Too often during implementation efforts, the participants don't spend enough time thinking about and negotiating the deliverable to be handed off. They proceed on the basis of just their own assumptions. The IC needs to help the participants *validate these assumptions* amongst themselves. During a JIP Test Planning Session the IC can say, "How many test scripts are you planning to write for each test case?" or "Why do you plan to write only two test scripts for each test case?" Misunderstandings of task scope and deliverables are rampant in every implementation, and tend to play hell with the implementation schedule. Depending on their extent, these misunderstandings may throw you way off the schedule. Therefore, the IC should continually ask questions that validate assumptions, eliminate ambiguity, and define deliverable hand-offs.

What someone believes they're getting and what another person thinks they're delivering are rarely the same.

—IC truism

Each person or group responsible for a deliverable should put their understanding of what is to be delivered in writing; this Work Statement is then included in the Implementation Workbook. Work Statements go a long way toward clarifying misunderstandings. It can be hard for some people to produce a Work Statement from scratch. People tend to be much better at refining or adapting a document than they are at creating a completely new one. So ICs usually ask people what they've used before for a Work Statement and then suggest modeling the current Work Statement upon the previous one. If they've never produced a Work Statement before, the IC can produce a *straw* Work Statement that gives them an idea of what is expected.

Once upon an implementation, the test scripts were written by the posting application because that group had all the information required to build a valid transaction for testing. However, the posting application happened to be at the end of the daily-batch job-stream. For their own testing, the upstream application groups had to code a number of programs to convert the test scripts into transactions that looked like they had just been captured. Needless to say, the test scripts delivered by the posting application group were not in a format that could be input into the special conversion programs coded by the upstream application groups. There was considerable consternation, but the fact of the matter was that some definitely invalid assumptions had been made. The IC had to jump into the fray to help expedite the process of getting the test scripts into a format that the upstream application groups could utilize. The IC became painfully aware that validating those assumptions beforehand would have been much easier than crunch-time gap-filling.

Deliverables

A *deliverable* is a completed, agreed-upon work item that a person or group hands off to another. What constitutes a deliverable is always open to considerable debate. The IC has to help the participants in the implementation achieve a negotiated settlement about what the deliverables are to be.

Once upon an implementation, the IC was facilitating the development of test cases in JIP Test Case Development Sessions. The system to be implemented was complex, necessitating numerous JIP Sessions. The business user became concerned and wondered out loud to the IC, "How much of my life do I have to devote to the programmers so that they can write these test scripts?" The business user was properly concerned because she had her own job to do, aside from assisting with the implementation of the new system. So the IC had to handle the negotiation process between the business user and the programmers of the test scripts. The issue was how much time the business user was willing to devote toward the development of test cases detailed enough for the programmers to build the test scripts. The IC knew that if the business user and programmers didn't reach agreement on the level of detail, they would get into a closed loop in which the business user would be saying, "Didn't we already do those test cases?" while the programmers would be saying, "We've found that the test cases developed to date don't test all the functionality within the system." The IC was able to impress upon both the programmers and the business user the importance of coming to an agreement about how detailed the test cases would be beforehand, so that everyone would understand what was expected of them.

The optimum situation is when the programmers and business users are willing to "go the extra mile" so that every misunderstanding about a deliverable can be resolved without undue consternation. However, in some implementations neither group is willing to work at meeting the other group halfway. As an IC, that's when you know you've got a tough job in front of you. You're going to have to spend much more time in the various JIP Sessions taking every detail of each deliverable down to a much finer level of granularity to make sure there are no omissions or misunderstandings.

You can't trust the person who is responsible for handing off a deliverable to tell you whether the work is done. You must ask the person who is the recipient of the deliverable. The recipient will tell you whether the work on the deliverable is really done. Many times, if you ask the person working on the deliverable whether or not their work is done, she will say, "Oh yea, that deliverable is done. I'm already talking to Julie (the recipient) about it." Then, a week later you run into Julie and she says, "That deliverable is only half-baked; there's absolutely no way I can work with it." At this point you must go back to the person responsible for the deliverable and say, "OK, it's time to get down. Your deliverable is either (1) not yet done, or (2) we're going to have to work something out with Julie."

It's best to conduct interactions about misunderstandings and miscommunications in JIP Sessions because it's much more effective than going one-on-one. When issues are discussed in the forum of a JIP Session, the participants get right to the core of the problem. No one can pass the buck when the other person with whom they're supposed to be working or interacting is in attendance. If you try to deal with the problem outside the JIP Session, you could waste all your time carrying the debate back and forth between the antagonists.

One caveat about deliverables. Sometimes what a group or a person delivers is all that can be achieved during the time allotted. In this kind of situation the IC has to make the recipient person or group realize that, given the circumstances, this is the most that can be accomplished. This is an example of how the IC can really expedite the implementation by reconciling the recipients to what they would otherwise perceive as an incomplete deliverable.

Monitoring Expectations

The problem with task accountability is that issues fall through the gaps between the tasks. These accountability issues are typically due to mismatched expectations about the deliverables. The IC must continually inquire about the implementation participants' *expectations* to make sure everybody either gets what they expected, or delivers what's expected of them. *Expectations change daily.* For example, an application group may find that the deliverable it expected to receive has components that are not the responsibility of the delivering group. These extraneous components are outside the delivering group's area of responsibility. As another example, one group may find that the volume of data it has been assigned to deliver won't be nearly enough for the recipient group to perform all of its testing. Mismatched expectations regarding a deliverable can be a source of major problems if they are not handled properly and forthrightly. One of the keys to an IC's success is constantly inquiring about everyone's expectations.

Once upon an implementation, an application group produced a Work Statement that detailed every test script that this group was going to write. However, there was a tremendous amount of detail and complexity in the computer programs—so much so that it was impossible to comprehend how much work the test scripts really entailed at the time the Work Statement was written. The programmers who wrote the Work Statement just didn't realize how many problems they were going to have building the test scripts until they physically got into the program code. However, because the IC kept inquiring about everyone's problems and concerns throughout the implementation, she was able to forestall any potential problems with mismatched expectations by informing the recipients of the test scripts about how those scripts would differ from what was promised in the Work Statement.

You can't always rely on project management software to show you the gaps in task accountability. Automated tools can deceive you into believing that you have accounted for everything when in fact you aren't there yet. ICs have found that as they examine a task more closely, they often realize that what they entered in their automated tool as one task is really twenty tasks. To find all the gaps in task accountability, you need to pay close attention—on an ongoing basis—to the issue of people's expectations.

Once upon an implementation, the IC drew a Gantt chart that showed the installation schedule for every office. The chart was color-coded and looked great. She thought she had everything well laid out. Each bar on the Gantt chart represented six weeks for each office installation. However, she hadn't broken the chart down any further than that. One evening as she was going home she stopped by the office of an implementation participant named Ted to inquire about his expectations and found out that he was very upset. The IC said, "We have the schedule; what else do you need?" Ted said, "There's not a fine-enough level of detail." Ted's team was responsible for the last task in each six-week office installation that was represented on the Gantt chart as a single bar. All the tasks that preceded Ted's were getting done late, yet everyone was pointing at Ted's team as the culprit in every late installation. Ted's team was in fact the only team getting their task done on time. However, there was no way to determine that by looking at the Gantt chart. What the IC had failed to delineate on the chart were the other tasks that had to be completed within their own time-frame or they would impact the whole schedule. When the installation fell behind schedule, Ted's team was left "holding the bag."

When Ted started screaming at the IC, she finally listened. The next morning she came to the office early and drew up a new Gantt chart that identified every task within each six-week period, along with the status of each deliverable of each group—at minus 90 days, minus 60 days, and so forth. Then the IC was able to track each discrete office-installation task and review these tasks every week in front of that group's boss. She would say, "You were supposed to have the cabling for the Local Area Network (LAN) installed by Tuesday of this week. Is it done or do you still have more work to do?" By taking the time to inquire about Ted's expectations, the IC was made aware of a major problem with the Gantt chart and how it didn't accurately differentiate each group's task accountability. After the IC resolved this problem, Ted and his team began to like her a lot more.

JIP Status Sessions

JIP Status Sessions are a forum for sharing information about the problems and progress of the implementation. The importance of sharing information is evident when one team discusses their progress toward their deliverable and then another team says, "Oh, I thought we were going to get that information from their file and we now see they aren't planning to give it to us." JIP Status Sessions can help catch these types of misunderstandings and invalid assumptions.

ICs don't make life easy for those people who choose to show up late or leave early from the JIP Status Sessions. For example, it's not your responsibility to chase after those people who were late or quick to leave, in order to inform them about what decisions were reached in that session. Since ICs rarely publish minutes of JIP Status Sessions, delinquents miss out on what was discussed. ICs find that once this tone is set, people don't like missing JIP Status Sessions because valuable information is being shared.

Many people really hate "status meetings" because, as a forum for information exchange, status meetings have really been abused. Sometimes it seems like status meetings are merely gatherings where the attendees are not straight about their concerns, the person in charge talks about whatever they want to talk about, and then the meeting is over. So the IC should reach out to everyone and let them know that the JIP Status Sessions are really different—they are truly an open exchange.

You can do this by asking, "Has anyone come upon anything in their work that we haven't thought of yet?" or "While you were driving into work this morning did you think of anything that I ought to note in the Implementation Workbook?" or "Is there anything we're not doing that we ought to be doing?"

ICs typically bring prepared material to JIP Status Sessions that updates everyone from where the implementation effort was last time to where it is at present. The IC then talks this material through. The Issues Log is reviewed at every JIP Status Session. If a new issue is identified, it goes into the Issues Log and may even get referred to a JIP Problem Solving Session. After reviewing the IC's prepared material and the Issues Log, each person or group participating in the JIP Status Session presents a quick overview of their efforts to date. Figure 8.7 is an example of a Status Report someone

---

STATUS REPORT   Page 1 of n

Implementation:	Date:

Presenter:

Presenter Phone Number:	E-Mail ID:

System/Application:

Tasks Completed:

Tasks Outstanding:

Open Issues:

Concerns:

Figure 8.7.   **JIP Status Session Report**

would present at a JIP Status Session. As part of their report the person or group should also express any issues they have with or concerns they have about the implementation.

ICs should keep track of who attends JIP Status Sessions and who doesn't, in case they need that information for political support in the future. For example, when a manager says, "Why didn't Joe know what was going on?" the IC can say, "Well, he never came to any JIP Status Sessions, so that might explain it; here are my attendance records."

Structure is a good thing and ICs try to bring structure to every implementation by holding the JIP Status Sessions at the same time and place every week. You should never change the time and place because it's important to establish consistency. ICs find that their initial JIP Status Sessions are typically an hour long but then as the implementation progresses, they try to shorten them to one-half hour or less. People are busy, so don't ask for any more of their time than is absolutely necessary.

CHAPTER 9

When an Implementation Goes Awry: Key Learnings

When an implementation goes awry, prepare yourself for an emotional rollercoaster—you'll have trouble sleeping at night, and you'll wake up second guessing every decision you've made on the implementation. This is the downside of the IC's job: the stress and psychic drain that goes along with system crashes. Although it's obviously appropriate to learn what you can from a situation and move on, it's only human nature to brood over your mistakes. Therefore, to survive as an IC, you need to practice some "centering techniques" so that you can deal with these occasional times of high stress.

> *Murphy's Law of Thermodynamics:*
> *Things get worse under pressure.*

CENTERING TECHNIQUES

Centering techniques are routines or diversions that you can use to maintain your peace of mind. Yogi masters speak of how the mind is a cage of chaotic monkeys, and the purpose of meditation is to get these rambunctious animals under control. While meditation is an excellent centering technique, it certainly isn't the only one.

Look at your life and see what has worked for you before. Getting out on those green links and playing golf, or maybe walking on

Figure 9.1.   **Centering for Peace of Mind**

the beach with your dog are both excellent for relaxation and centering. What's important is to have some routine or diversion to occupy you during those times when your mind won't let you alone. Figure 9.1 is a symbolic representation of "centering" the mind.

A CASE HISTORY

The following sections tell one IC's story of how an implementation went awry. The IC felt so guilty she wanted to leave town and change her name, but by keeping "centered," she was able to deal with this stressful situation.

The Situation.   The Implementation Plan called for the product to be installed in two stages. In the first stage, the specialty items would be installed in the inventory database. In the second stage, after stabilization of the inventory processing, the commodity items would be installed in the inventory database. The senior management personnel felt they could reduce their risk by implementing one type of item into the inventory processing at a time.

The items being introduced to the inventory database involved multi-cycle processing. Multi-cycle processing means that transactions against these items could not be completed in one business day (one batch run). On Day One, an electronic transaction for an item is received and posted against the inventory database. On the second day, the paper copy of that same transaction is received and must match the electronic transaction—otherwise the paper will post as a new transaction against the inventory database. So if a paper copy is not received that matches the electronic transaction, then the electronic transaction received on the first day must be reversed off the inventory database. The reversals go into the third day's cycle. So a given transaction could be processing for three cycles (days).

What made this implementation especially difficult was the large number of application-program changes that needed to be made to support the electronic capture and posting of the transactions, matching the paper copies against the electronic transactions, and generating reversals for non-matching transactions. Within the multi-cycle processing, the most difficult aspect was the second day. (The first-day posting of the electronic transactions was pure vanilla.) It was on the second day—when the paper copies had to be matched against the electronic transactions from Day One and, if necessary, reversals generated—that the real complexity of the implementation was encountered.

Multiple Contingencies. When you're implementing a multi-cycle process, you need a well thought out and documented contingency plan for backing out each cycle. It is standard procedure in most organizations that nothing is implemented without a contingency plan for backing out whatever's being installed. This implementation had explicit instructions and procedures for backing out the installation after Day One of the multi-process cycle. However, the implementation got into trouble on the second day. The backout procedures for Day One were not valid for the second day of the multi-cycle process. Backing out the installation on Day Two would have impacted over 10,000 items on the inventory database.

When you do organization-wide implementations you can get

caught in the mind-set that says, "We must go forward. There is no retreat," which is your basic "death-march" scenario. This is what happened to the IC and consequently she didn't look prudently at contingencies for resolving every possible variation of backing out a complex multi-cycle process. She should have called a JIP Contingency Planning Session for each processing day with every application group that was participating in the implementation. Information systems are so interdependent that every application needs to be represented to make sure a comprehensive backout plan is developed. At the JIP Contingency Planning Session, a strategy could have been mapped out for handling every application in the event of a failure on any of the three separate cycles of the process. Sometimes developing contingencies to this extent may necessitate writing new programs with no other function than to support an application's backout. However, it's better to expend the effort writing and testing these programs beforehand than to have a team of programmers writing them at four o'clock in the morning, which was what this implementation had to do.

Recovery

After installation changes have been backed-out, you then have to recover all the files and databases. As part of the JIP Contingency Planning, make sure every application can properly handle files and databases with no data. During recovery you will definitely have empty files being passed through the batch run. This implementation had a very difficult time with recovery because some of the application programs couldn't accept empty files being handed-off from another application.

Victims of History

Over the years, this particular organization had developed an unwritten policy that all installations were done on Friday night. The rationale behind this policy is obvious. If anything went wrong, you had all weekend free to work your butt off to clean up the mess. One of the IC's first mistakes was in acceding to this policy without really thinking through all its implications for her particular implementation.

As part of the implementation the business users had a new online system installed, with which they could control the flow of the electronic transactions into the batch run. In the Post-Implementation Review of the bungled implementation, it was suggested that the implementation should have installed the programming changes and online system on Friday night and then turned on the flow of the electronic transactions the next week on Thursday night. This would have given the implementation participants time to determine whether any application system was getting hit by the extensive changes and the new system installed. Then Day One of the multi-cycle process could have been started by the business users, releasing the flow of electronic transactions on the next Thursday night. This way, the difficult Day Two of the multi-cycle process would have been on Friday night, giving the implementation participants all weekend to correct anything that went wrong.

By not thinking through the implementation and all its implications, the IC became a prisoner of the organization's history. The lesson she learned was don't be a victim of the prevailing mental models. View every implementation as unique and make no assumptions.

Mental models are deeply held images of how the world works. These images limit us to familiar ways of thinking and acting.

—Peter Senge

The Problem

Following the organization's standard operating procedure (SOP), the IC, the application programmers, and the database administrators were on site Friday night for Day One of the installation. They monitored the batch process as it was executing with the changes to the program code, the job control language (JCL), the job scheduler, the security package, and so forth. Everything went smoothly, with just the usual JCL hiccups. Monday night everyone was back on site to monitor once again the batch process for Day Two of the multi-cycle process.

All the implementation's problems began on Monday night, the second day of the multi-cycle process. Mr. Gogonow (<u>Go</u>tta <u>go</u> <u>now</u>)—the designer and programmer for the Here Comes Trouble (HCT) application—had been planning a vacation trip to Ixtapa, Mexico, for over a year. Gogonow's manager decided not to ask him

to give up his vacation because he had been planning it for so long. The manager figured that the installation of the application's changes could be done without Gogonow. And so this application's key resource—who did all the design and coding for the HCT application—was on vacation instead of being on site. The person they did have on site instead was Mr. IdbIc (I'm doing the best I can), who did all the HCT-application JCL changes and executed all the test scripts through the HCT-application test-kit in support of the implementation. Although IdbIc understood the HCT application, he was in no position to go digging into the program language looking for coding problems. The implementation had already had problems with the HCT application during the Joint Integration Testing. So the fact that there were problems on Monday night during installation was not a surprising revelation.

The IC had no authority to tell Gogonow's manager, "You can't let this guy go to Mexico now when we need him here." However, the IC did state her opinion by saying, "I don't think that letting the HCT designer go on vacation at this time is a good idea." She instinctively knew it could lead to bad things. Then she asked the manager, "Who are you going to have there on site with IdbIc during the installation?" The manager said, "Oh, I believe IdbIc can cover it by himself." To which the IC replied, "I think you should have someone else on site to assist IdbIc. There are at least fifteen people in this organization who have worked on this application in the past. If you don't know who they are then I can help find one of them for you." Due only to the IC's pushing and prodding, the manager finally did get someone to work with Mr. IdbIc during the installation. Incredibly, he picked someone who had never worked on the application before!

What Happened

Early Monday evening the HCT application abended (abnormally terminated). Mr. IdbIc and his assistant read *what they thought* was a Return Code telling them that a database table was out of space. So IdbIc had the database administrator increase the table's space and restarted the batch cycle from the latest checkpoint. As the restarted job was executing, the IC started getting calls from the downstream applications saying they were abending with transactions that referenced non-existent inventory items. The data being passed between the applications was supposed to contain transactions that referenced only existing inventory items. IdbIc and his assistant now believed that when the space problem occurred, the database management system corrupted the pointers into the database table—and because of these corrupted pointers, the restart at the checkpoint had shipped invalid transactions downstream. IdbIc suggested the entire batch cycle be rerun from the beginning of the logical day to correct both the database-table space problem and the corrupted pointers.

The IC assembled the Installation Management Team at midnight to make sure that the implementation was in compliance with organizational procedures and that she had the authorization to rerun the entire batch cycle. On the second run of the batch cycle, the HCT application abended with exactly the same error. IdbIc and his assistant now believed the problem was a newly installed product that preallocated all buffers (the storage caches for read-and-write processing). If the IC could just get the authority to turn the preallocation product off, IdbIc said the database table would have enough memory to execute the job. By now it was obvious to the IC that as IdbIc and his assistant pulled ideas out of the air, they were creating a whirlwind of trouble for her!

The IC (and everyone else on site) knew it would be a problem to try to back out the installation due to the multi-cycle process. The consensus feeling was that they should give the database table enough "gas" (space) to get a clean execution of the batch cycle; then at least the company could conduct its business as usual when the office opened on Tuesday morning. It would also buy them time to figure out how to correct the problem before the batch cycle started the next evening. So the database administrator increased the table's space even more, the IC got the preallocation product turned off, and the entire batch cycle was rerun. The HCT application finally did reach completion without abending, but by now it was early Tuesday morning.

After the HCT application had executed, the IC insisted that the database be checked to make sure there weren't any transactions that referenced non-existent inventory items. To the IC's disgust and dismay, the database did contain invalid transactions. The downstream applications were abending. It was now evident to everyone that the implementation had a serious problem. The batch cycle for Monday was not done and no one had a clue regarding what was wrong with the HCT application. The implications were enormous. It looked liked the company would not be able to process orders when it opened for business that day. People started "going ballistic." It was scary. This is when the IC really began to question whether being an IC was a good career choice.

Solving the Wrong Problem

The IC was finally able to bring more expertise to bear on the problem and it was discovered that Mr. IdbIc and his assistant *had misunderstood* the Return Code. The Return Code wasn't from the database management system but was in fact generated by the application program. It's easy to say that the Return Codes from two disparate

sources should be as different as apples and oranges. However, since Mr. IdbIc and his assistant weren't familiar with the programming language it was impossible for them to differentiate between the two Return Codes. What the Return Code was really saying was that the application program itself was out of space, not the database table. The program was running out of space because it was generating too many records. It had been generating both valid and invalid transactions. IdbIc and his assistant had spent the entire evening solving the wrong problem. This was all because the IC could not bring the key resource to bear on the problem. As the organization was getting burned, Mr. Gogonow—the person who would have immediately understood the arcane Return Code—was also getting burned on the beach in Ixtapa.

Command Centers

By now the organization was in escalation mode, because it was evident that there had been a major disaster. The IC began the process of setting up command centers at various locations around the organization. The implementation had its own command center for the installation, and the IC piggy-backed onto the organization's existing infrastructure for disaster recovery to set up the other command centers. The IC coordinated and facilitated a JIP Disaster Recovery Session with all the other command centers on conference calls. There were a lot of people involved in these JIP Sessions because the problem had impacted every downstream application. The organization was at a virtual standstill for any information systems processing. The sales representatives in the field were trying to hold the line by saying, "We can take your order but we can't confirm it, nor can we verify our inventory levels to determine if it is in stock." Senior management was not happy.

JIP Disaster Recovery Sessions

The Project Manager chaired and the IC facilitated the JIP Disaster Recovery Sessions. The IC said, "Here's the situation. We don't know what the problem is. We don't know if the data is any good." The process was to talk through all the problems. The IC utilized the Session Boards to assist in brainstorming for ideas and then she strove for consensus on the best strategy. There were some issues on which the session participants just could not reach unanimity, so to expedite the process the IC had to resort to voting. The JIP Disaster Recovery Sessions were held every two hours around the clock. Approximately 35 people were in each JIP Session, with the other command centers on conference call. There were six different teams writing programs to support the recovery.

JIP Disaster Recovery Session:
1. *Discuss* the problem.
2. *Assess* the damage.
3. *Decide* what has to be done.
4. *Determine* what are the risks.
5. *Prioritize* the recovery procedures.

The recovery was much more difficult than anything the organization had attempted before. Everyone was working extemporaneously because they just weren't prepared for such a disaster. The IC tried to maintain the focus of the participants so that the JIP Sessions didn't degenerate into shouting and finger pointing.

Post-Implementation Review

After the recovery was completed and the organization was once again functioning in a normal mode of operation, the postmortem reviews began. These postmortems were called the Post-Implementation Reviews. In setting up the facilities for these reviews, it's important to create an environment in which the participants can feel safe, supported, and free to talk. Although the IC coordinated the Post-Implementation Reviews—and certainly had input on the format, content, and list of attendees—the reviews were chaired by the managers of the business units. It was felt that the IC shouldn't facilitate these reviews because she was a key player in the installation, the disaster, and the recovery. A number of people expressed an interest in attending the Post-Implementation Review. However, those people who had not participated in the actual installation and recovery were not invited. It was felt that those people who were non-participants had nothing to contribute and could just read the review notes for any informational background they desired.

There were two Post-Implementation Reviews. The first review focused on the time-frame that included when the problem first occurred up to the point at which the IC knew the implementation was a major disaster. The second review focused on the time-frame from the acknowledgment of the disaster until the organization's information systems were fully recovered. The Project Manager insisted that the reviews be segregated this way because she didn't want to solve the organization's problems of dealing with a disaster. The Project Manager wanted the first review to deal just with the problems pertinent to the implementation.

The second Post-Implementation Review was about how the organization dealt with the disaster. This involved how the command centers were initiated, how the escalation was handled (for example, whether the right managers were notified in a timely manner), and whether the people in authority had the correct information on which to act. The organization had rigorous procedures in place for power outages, earthquakes, and riots in the streets. They also had standard procedures for an implementation problem within one application. What they didn't have was a process for recovering from a blown implementation impacting all the information systems within the organization. This implementation was installing a cooperative processing architecture across the organization's numerous heterogeneous platforms. Therefore, the goal of the second review was to produce a document that specified procedures for dealing with such a disaster in the future.

Acknowledging Blunders

The IC felt it was crucial to her credibility at the Post-Implementation Review to admit her mistakes. So at the review she said, "I didn't have a multiple contingency plan for all the batch cycles, and clearly that was needed." When that was noted as an action item, the IC said that item belonged to her. The IC wanted to exhibit responsibility and dignity by coming clean, "copping to" her errors in judgment, and acknowledging her blunders.

The IC also went to the Project Manager and said, "I blew the implementation. If it makes your position any easier to fire me or ask for my resignation, please do so. I won't be angry or get weird. I take responsibility for my actions and can handle the consequences." But the Project Manager asked the IC to stay on, and then commended the IC for the way in which she had handled the emergency. The Project Manager knew what a tough job it is to coordinate a motley crew of programmers, managers, and business users—each with their own agendas and priorities.

The Error

This implementation failure was so big that it was reported in the newspaper. And what was the error that brought the organization to a standstill? It was simply that a three-dimensional array wasn't big enough to hold all the records for an internal program-sort. This minor oversight brought down 36 information systems across the entire organization.

Key Resources

The biggest problem with the implementation was that the IC didn't have the right people working on it at the right time. Mr. IdbIc and his assistant were no substitute for Mr. Gogonow. A second problem was with the application testing. The manager for the HCT application did not take personal responsibility of making sure that it was fully tested. The manager told IdbIc to test only selected test-cases with the test-kit. Although the IC stressed full testing of every test-case for each application and documented that in the Implementation Plan, she was still dependent on each application's manager to see that this was accomplished. There is no way the IC could ensure that this was done because she didn't know the applications well enough to question the managers intelligently about each test-case. If the managers said they had tested everything, the IC had to take their word for it. The third problem was that senior management refused to fund Joint Dry Run Testing, which probably would have found the problem.

Push and Pull

One of the *key learnings* for the IC was this: when you have an implementation that is cross-organizational and you are dependent on many systems to produce a piece and do their job, you must be able to sense and then look for the weak link. The IC knew that the HCT application was her weak link in the implementation effort. Most of the "bugs" (programming problems) that were found during integration testing were in the HCT code, and every date that was missed was because of the HCT application group. The IC also knew that she had a problem with the manager in charge. Therefore, the IC had to make a judgment call. Should she go along with this manager's assurances that everything was OK, or should she challenge the manager? It comes down to a matter of "push and pull." As the IC, she had no authority over this manager. So how much could she *push* the manager to do what she believed to be right? And how much *pull* could she exert to get the manager moving in the right direction? Could she trust him to do his job, or should she just get in his face and say, "You're not doing your job." These were tough judgment calls. When the IC had asked Mr. Gogonow (the programmer doing the coding), "How's it going?" he replied that he needed two more weeks of testing. Despite this fact, the manager said everything was fine, the implementation should go ahead as planned, and then sent his key resource to another country! The IC had to decide whether the programmer's concerns were valid or whether the manager knew better. She made the wrong decision. She trusted the manager.

Let's Get It Right

Before the HCT application group (that had bungled the implementation) retested the system to validate their solution to the problems, the IC assembled a JIP Test Planning Session to make sure that every piece of the HCT application would in fact be tested. By now the IC had lots of political capital because the HCT application group had blown the implementation. The IC was empowered to do whatever she felt was needed to make sure that the HCT application was thoroughly tested, regardless of what the manager said. The JIP Test Planning Session consisted of skilled technicians from other applications who provided their input on how best to test. At the end of the JIP Session the IC told the HCT application manager, "It's your team's job to take all this good information, think about it, and then come back to this group with a plan of how you're going to test your system. And you have to get everyone in this JIP Session to sign off your plan." In addition to facilitating the JIP Test Planning Session, the IC did help the manager negotiate for the support needed from other application groups in order to conduct the testing.

CONCLUSION

Although it took over 18 hours to find the implementation problem and several days to get the batch cycle back on time, control of the information systems was never lost, not one purchase order was butchered, not one item of inventory was unaccounted for, and the general ledger was never one cent out-of-balance. Given the complexity of the implementation (36 information systems, 11 million inventory items, and multi-cycle processing), the senior management ended up satisfied with the IC and her efforts.

CHAPTER **10**

Politicking: A Survival and Success Guide

The key to being a successful Implementation Coordinator is the ability to influence people to do what needs to be done. This is the *art of politicking*—influencing circumstances beyond your direct control. Every implementation is afflicted with bureaucratic rigidity, personality conflicts, technical complexity, and resource scarcity. Therefore, the IC needs to politick so as to minimize the impact of these disruptive influences on the implementation and its participants.

Politicking is different from *playing politics*—which means influencing the decision-making process to the detriment of the product or system to be implemented. There is a fine line between being effective at politicking and playing politics—a line that can create an ethical dilemma. What's right and wrong is something you have to decide for yourself.

> *For whatsoever a man soweth, that shall he also reap.*
>
> *—St. Paul, Epistle to the book of Galatians*

The way to build your influence within an organization is through networking. Figure 10.1 is a symbolic representation of the networking you must do to achieve any influence. Salespeople nowadays can't function without contact-management software on their computers, and as an IC, it's a good idea for you to have some sort of similar mechanism for personal networking. It doesn't have

Figure 10.1.   **Network/Influence Wheel**

to be automated or computerized. For example, you could maintain your Contact List in a loose-leaf binder, or even a notebook. Your contact list should obviously note each person's name, phone number, e-mail ID, and so forth. However, it could also contain space for writing notes about the person's preferences and concerns within the organization, and interests and responsibilities outside of it. How do you learn these things? By asking people directly. This demonstrates that you are interested in everyone, not just for their functional responsibilities within the organization, but more broadly as human beings. This doesn't have to be disingenuous. As noted way back in the Introduction, an IC is a person who genuinely likes working with people. Finding out about people's lives—their preferences and peeves, their avocations and families—is also a constant source of amazement, just because people are amazing if you take the time to know them.

Moreover, people's preferences within the organization, their style and manner, are what they themselves feel is important to their organization and their professional image. For example, one person might feel that becoming vice-president within the next three years is her professional goal, and the hallmark of professional success. As an IC, knowing this information is useful; it tells you this person's "hot button." You can influence her by pointing out that supporting your implementation might promote her goal. Another person might believe that for the business to be successful it must employ the principles of Total Quality Management (TQM). Again, you can gain influence by having your implementation adhere to the fundamentals of Total Quality Management.

Knowing a person's interests outside the organization—their hobbies and spare-time activities—isn't enough for the IC. It pays to invest some time to learn something about the person's particular avocation. For example, many an IC has weakened her professional position by maintaining a personal attitude about a hobby she feels is ridiculous or inconsequential. Sports is a classic example. Many people are "turned-off" by professional sports, perceiving them to be trivial or boring. In fact, interest in sports is one of the greatest of

Once upon an implementation, the work effort was running on a very tight schedule. Alfredo, the Quality Assurance (QA) person who was responsible for every implementation change installed into the production environment, happened to be an opera buff. Although the IC didn't know opera from operator, she did know it was in her best interest to "talk opera;" so she learned the names of some major performers—like Placido Domingo and Luciano Pavarotti—and the offerings on this season's bill at the opera house—*La Bohème, La Traviata, and Lucia di Lammermoor* (such delightful arias). This not-too-difficult research paid off when a component of the implementation had to be changed at the last minute, without enough time to fulfill all the organization's standard procedures. But the IC, who had previously chit-chatted with Alfredo about opera in the hallways and cafeteria, now went to his office with some influence that she could exert. Alfredo, as QA, didn't view the IC as just another nerd wanting to circumvent the rules, but rather as a kindred music lover in need of help. While they were discussing the opera currently in town, the Quality Assurance person installed the IC's changes.

all social equalizers, a great medium of exchange between people of all kinds. The ability to "talk sports" provides a vehicle for people of completely dissimilar backgrounds to have animated and lengthy conversations, which in turn builds friendships and fosters business relationships.

In politicking as in salesmanship, *timing is everything*. If you're late, the decision has already been made. If you're early, you have no impact. You have to pick your shot and be lucky. You won't always win.

Some days you eat the bear. Some days the bear eats you.

—*Anonymous*

To politick effectively you must be sensitive to people and their circumstances. Never minimize the value of "small talk" and its impact on your influence with someone. Take the time to converse with, and say something relevant and positive to each implementation participant. This requires thought on your part and maybe even some background reading. Go ahead; improve your mind. This is how your Contact List will prove invaluable.

POLITICAL CAPITAL

Political capital refers to the people-assets that you as an IC possess or control. These assets can take many forms: influence, authority, leverage, knowledge, charisma. However, you must remember that, like Cinderella at the ball, these assets are finite. At "midnight," or some other crucial point in time, you may suddenly discover that these assets have been depleted—so don't spend your political capital carelessly and then expect to be bailed out by an equivalent of the glass slipper. It seldom happens. The hardest part of having political capital is deciding when and where to invest or "burn" it. It's a judgment call. Obviously, you want to use your political capital only when it's really necessary. However, you will agonize over not having used it when, in hindsight, you think you should have—and you will beat yourself up when you don't have enough political capital left and you desperately need it. Making these decisions is one of the tricky parts of being an IC.

BUILDING A CONSTITUENCY

All organizations are made up of political factions. The IC can shape the political dynamics of the organization by building a constituency of people and groups to support her implementation. The IC must determine who she can enlist, persuade, offer incentives to, or avoid in building her constituency.

When Looking for Constituents Ask These Questions:
1. Who can make it happen?
2. Who can help it happen?
3. Who will let it happen?
4. Who will get in the way?

> *Placate the people you can't avoid and avoid the people you can't placate.*
>
> *—Guy Kawasaki*

DOING THE RIGHT THING

How much can you pressure people and groups within the organization to make them do the right thing? This is one of the classic dilemmas that confronts an IC. You know what should be done; the issue is: How much of your political capital do you want to spend to gain that objective? More important, does it even matter? One of the ironies of life in this business is that you can do all the wrong things and still succeed. Taking the methodical and comprehensive approach to an implementation only increases the likelihood that it will go well. It doesn't guarantee it. Conversely, running the implementation by the seat of your pants doesn't guarantee that it will fail. So you have to "hedge your bets" and insist on those objectives that you feel are critical to the implementation, while letting other objectives slide—even against your better judgment. You can't have everything your way. Of course, if the objective you let slide "burns" you during the implementation, you'll never forgive yourself. It has happened to every IC a few times and they have all spent sleepless nights asking themselves, "Why didn't I *insist* on that objective?"

CULTURAL CONSTRAINTS

An organization's "culture" consists of its history and the work habits of the organizational personnel. The culture of an organization dominates every aspect of the implementation. It is a constant source of discussion amongst an IC and her colleagues because it helps them understand why it can be so difficult to get some things done. An organization's culture and its constraints are realities that must be worked through; sometimes they're annoying, sometimes they help.

Everyone is a prisoner of the organization's culture. For example, if the organization's culture condones the situation that nothing ever gets done on time, then the IC inherits that constraint. To transcend cultural constraints, ICs start by educating some of the implementation participants about how they can improve their work habits (what you really mean is to *change* their work habits, but you don't want to call it that). ICs point out, in a friendly way, what people could do to excel at their jobs. The IC might say, "These test cases will get approved faster if you take leadership at this point" or "The implementation could use your direction in getting these programming changes made before there is trouble downstream." The idea is to define various roles, choose people to fill them, and then help those you've chosen to play the roles. The IC builds on the efforts of a select few people to convince a larger number of others to exceed their inculcated cultural constraints.

TRANSCENDING INERTIA

Rest assured that as an IC you'll find yourself from time to time in the awkward situation of not knowing the right thing to do. You look for an opening to step forward and say something, but you can't seem to find the right opportunity. What you're dealing with is "implementation inertia," or resistance to action or change. Usually this is because your *role is ill-defined.* You want to be the implementation's coordinator but no one else sees you in that capacity or understands the role. Politically this is a ticklish situation. Becoming an irritant is the best you can initially hope for. Try asking "What are you going to do about this?" or "What about that issue?"

Networking is one way to transcend inertia. On every implementation you will find that people are either part of the solution or part of the problem. Try taking those persons who are (or could be) part of the solution to lunch, in order to express your support for them and their agenda. Plant a seed of solution in their heads. Conversely, try taking those persons who are part of the problem to lunch, in order to point out strengths among the implementation participants that they haven't really begun to tap. Try to assess how much resistance you're dealing with from each implementation participant. This information will help you make more intelligent decisions. If someone is totally entrenched, then it's hopeless. You must wait for a window of opportunity, which usually takes the form of either key persons moving on, or something really awful happening.

WORKING THE ORGANIZATION

Working the organization means knowing who to "cozy up to," who to placate, who to visit when you're out in the field, who to escalate your problems to, and so forth. The IC makes every effort to learn who the key people are within the organization, what they expect, and how they can help and/or hurt the implementation. How do you find out this kind of information? By communicating with anyone and everyone, and making mental notes as well as written ones. Remember that every organization has two organizational structures: a formal structure that is invariably a hierarchy consisting of teams, groups, departments, and divisions; and an informal structure that is best characterized as a network driven by who likes whom, who respects whom, and who listens to whom. Informal structures also consist of alliances or camps, such as the true believers in CASE tools, or the data bigots who hold the process-lovers in contempt. Anyone can learn the formal structure by referring to an organizational chart. However, as the IC, you need to ferret out the informal structure, which can be just as important, if not more so, than the formal structure. Once you've deciphered the informal structure and who's who in the hierarchy, you deliberately and judiciously *work the organization*. This is a process that continues throughout the entire implementation effort and beyond. Remember, you're building your own network for your next implementation while you're working on the current one.

GETTING ON SOMEONE ELSE'S AGENDA

One means of working the organization is to broadcast your implementation by scheduling speaking time on the staff meeting agenda of those application groups or service areas impacted by your

implementation. The IC and her Project Manager go to these staff meetings to present their implementation objectives and due dates. This ensures that each group and area understands what your implementation is doing, and that, politically speaking, you've "touched all the bases." It's always a good idea to say, "Let's go around the room and have everyone tell us how they view their own roles in our implementation. That will also tell me who to deal with in this group regarding specific issues that may impact either our implementation or your own area."

MANAGING NEGOTIATIONS

The IC must manage the negotiations between the business partners and the developers regarding the defining of deliverables and when they will be implemented. If you lose control of this process, it can have devastating consequences for the implementation. Organizations invite trouble if they let the business users ask the developers to change functionality within the system after a testing milestone for those particular functions has been achieved. If the developers are allowed to modify these functions, the milestones could be rendered irrelevant. Of course, the business users can submit Change Requests for legitimate changes to a system that is not yet implemented. The point is that the IC must coordinate the negotiation process in order to maintain the validity of the milestones. This can be done by retesting any functions that have been modified, or at least alerting the responsible parties to the fact that changes have been made. What you don't want are undisciplined technicians casually telling the business users, "Sure, we can do that"—and then proceeding to change the already tested code over the weekend. Don't laugh; it happens all the time!

> *If the test milestones have no credibility, then the testing effort has no reliability.*
>
> —*IC truism*

LOBBYING

The IC must lobby with senior management to get all the technical specialists necessary to the implementation effort to attend the JIP Sessions. The most valuable technical specialists within any organization are highly prized and sought after by everyone for good reason. These key people have the expertise and/or knowledge of the resident applications to make or break any project. As the JIP Session coordinator, you must schedule very carefully and lobby senior management to make sure these critical people are in attendance. Without them your JIP Sessions could be a waste of time for those participants who do attend. Lobbying senior management is necessary because resources as valuable as key technical specialists tend to respond only to the dictates of their senior managers.

INTRIGUE

Political intrigue is everywhere. Secretive scheming to effect change is well documented; for example, it can be found throughout Shakespeare's plays. The temptation to employ intrigue can be irresistible to an IC who is anxious to promote change. However, you've got to be concerned about destabilizing the situation and possibly even instigating chaos. Although you may want to affect the direction of the implementation, you don't want to—and can't afford to—sidestep the Project Manager or whatever procedures are currently in place. ICs, by the very nature of their role, are *agents of change,* because implementing anything is a change from the way business has been done in the past. What ICs find most effective is to promote change with friendly persuasion and positive reinforcement, not intrigue. It's noteworthy that the characters in Shakespeare's plays who rely on intrigue can never control the forces of their own creation.

Although ICs typically don't initiate intrigue, sometimes they are confronted by it. Someone may be secretly scheming to foil your implementation. It's best not to react to intrigue. Otherwise you could end up like Brer Fox in the Joel C. Harris classic, *Brer Rabbit and the Wonderful Tar Baby*. Once Brer Fox put his fist into the Tar Baby, it became impossible for him to extricate himself. It's the same with political intrigue. The more you get into it, the messier it becomes—and if you let it, it can drive you crazy. It's better to stay above the fray, and let your integrity and performance speak for themselves.

POLITICAL BACKBITING

Political backbiters attempt to undermine a person or project to promote their own position of power or personal agenda. Since ICs move throughout an entire organization to coordinate an implementation, they fall victim to backbiters and are accused of being backbiters themselves. Those who would backbite an IC are typically political vipers who tend to be ineffective performers. Don't dignify their slander with an injured response because poor performers always get found out. As for accusations of being a backbiter, you must ask yourself whether what you're doing is politically motivated, or are you really trying to get the product or system implemented? If you're working toward the implementation then you have to "suffer the slings and arrows of outrageous fortune" and trust that your good work won't go unrewarded.

IMPLEMENTATION POLITICS

In every implementation, ICs encounter political situations. While the circumstances are unique, the inherent problems aren't. Someone is annoyed, feels slighted, thinks they're being threatened, and so forth. Typically, it comes down to a misunderstanding or lack of communication. While in many instances political problems seem trifling (especially in regard to other major issues the IC has to resolve), it's important to deal with these problems in a forthright and timely manner. Otherwise minor political annoyances can balloon into major implementation problems.

Once upon an implementation, the IC had a colleague who received a promotion putting him in charge of the corporate information systems architecture. In his new capacity as Systems Architect (SA), this person questioned the IC's implementation. The SA wanted to know why the implementation was installing a new front-end for data capture instead of going through the existing one used by every other application within the corporation. The IC and Project Manager had good business reasons for installing a new front-end, which had to do with timing issues and making the new product's processing window. Also, the issue of a new front-end for data capture had been hammered out in numerous Joint Application Development (JAD) Sessions—which the Systems Architect hadn't attended because he had another job when those JAD Sessions were held.

The IC provided the SA with the literature from the JAD Sessions documenting the business case for a new front-end. The Systems Architect wasn't satisfied, so the IC offered to provide him with more information. The IC then requested the developers of the new front-end to provide the Systems Architect with a more complete answer. When the IC followed up the issue a week later, she found that the Systems Architect had not received the information requested. The IC again went to the developers, and this time rattled their cages by saying, "Hey, wake up; the Systems Architect needs a complete description of this issue in writing." The developers responded by dashing off a brief memo justifying the new front-end, which they e-mailed to the Systems Architect. Being on the distribution list, the IC also received a copy of the memo, and knew this reply was not going to be sufficient. So the IC went to the developers a third time, and told them she didn't think their response was going to satisfy the Systems Architect.

Their description was too short, lacked depth, and didn't show any analysis. The developers told the IC that the description was fine and nothing else would be required. The IC then escalated the issue to the developers' boss, who backed her developers by agreeing with them that the memo as it stood should suffice. The IC pointed out that the Systems Architect had to be taken seriously because he was being conservative in his new job. She then posed the question, "What if he make an issue of this?" The developers and their boss said they were still comfortable with their effort, so the IC backed off. She figured, "OK, if I hear from the SA that he isn't satisfied, then I will really take it on."

Well, the next thing the IC heard from the Systems Architect was that he had called for an Architectural Review of the entire implementation, which at this point was only three weeks away from the installation date. The IC was really bugged because she now had a major political problem on her hands merely because the Systems Architect's questions weren't answered thoroughly. The Systems Architect in his new position wanted to make sure that what was being implemented served the corporation's best interests. Therefore, he was going to put questions before an audience to find out why the implementation was building a new front-end.

The IC now made the System Architect's concerns a major priority. She met with him and tried to provide better answers, and promised to get him some of the benchmarked data that supported the business case. The IC also attempted to modify his position about the architecture. Although the Systems Architect was a techno-purist, the IC wanted him to understand that the design developed in the JAD Sessions was a compromise to fit the situation. The IC also escalated the issue to the senior manager of the developers, and reported that the implementation had a major problem because the issue was now going to be addressed in a public forum that could easily delay the implementation. The senior manager assured the IC that her staff was prepared for such a presentation. When the IC informed the Project Manager about the Architectural Review, she adamantly refused to participate, saying it was all a political gambit.

Aside from wasting a lot of people's time, the real danger in the Architectural Review was that the issues being raised would have to be addressed, whether credible or not. After pointing out to the Project Manager that the SA never got a good answer to his questions, the IC got the Project Manager to escalate the issue to the Systems Architect's senior manager and present the business case. In that meeting, the IC pointed out that every other group within the organization had reviewed and approved the implementation design. Upon further review the senior manager let the implementation design stand, canceling the Architectural Review.

If all else had failed, the IC (at the Project Manager's behest) could still have simply refused to participate in the Architectural Review, by just "stonewalling" it. However, while an effective tactic, stonewalling can create political animosities if not enemies, and is not recommended even as a last resort. It would be better to just bull through the Architectural Review, having done your homework, and then come out with all guns blazing. By having all the answers and data at your fingertips, you can murder the opposition with competence and thoroughness. "Overkill" is the recommended response.

How to Handle a Political Situation:

- Try to understand the other person's perspective.
- Try to redirect or remonstrate with the person.
- Escalate to the boss and say, "Is this really necessary?"
- Be prepared to defend your business case in public.

THE WALL

A common phenomenon witnessed by ICs on implementations within large organizations is called "the wall." This phenomenon occurs when a group in the organization draws a line around what it considers to be its area of responsibility. The area the group defines as its responsibility is typically very small, and between this

area and the rest of the organization stands "the wall." Although the fact that a wall exists is unspoken, its presence is evident to anyone who deals with that group. Not only is it difficult for the IC to get that group to accept responsibility for anything its people perceive to be outside their narrowly defined area, but they also have a nasty habit of tossing any tasks they don't choose to do "over the wall," claiming that it's someone else's obligation. Dealing with the wall causes ICs a lot of head-bumping.

Once upon an implementation, the IC worked for ABC Inc., a large institution that captured and distributed all its electronic data through one super information system known as WUYS (Without Us You're Screwed). WUYS was the main roadblock to any implementation within the corporation because it was everybody's favorite system, and groups were continually filling up the WUYS queues with both trifling and mission-critical features or products they wanted.

One of the logical features that WUYS was supposed to design to support the IC's implementation was a history update providing additional information about a transaction after it had already been processed. What this meant was adding some bytes to the history record. However, overlaying any existing bytes with the additional history wasn't feasible—WUYS had a limitation on its record size because all the records were blocked to fit on a particular physical device. Also, the timing of the updates was awkward because, once a transaction was processed and WUYS had built the history, having to update that file again meant a rearchitecture of their system. Needless to say, the WUYS group didn't want to change the record size or redesign their architecture.

So WUYS designed a separate file to contain the additional history. Then they started saying, "Well, since it's a separate file, are we the only ones that need to build it?" Suggesting that some other group build the file was WUYS group's way of putting up the wall. Now WUYS could just be a delivery system, and not maintain the history files for all the other systems in the corporation. So WUYS unilaterally took an architectural stand that said, "We are now a delivery system, and we are not going to do any enhancements to or build any more histories." Since the design of the file was complete, the issue came down to who was going to build it. The IC found herself in a bind due to the wall the WUYS group had created.

How does a development issue (such as who will build a file) end up in the IC's lap? You might be surprised to learn that it happens all the time. Issues that should get resolved early in the Systems Development Life Cycle float around until the IC swings into action and starts *forcing the issues*. By identifying the issue, the IC ends up owning it—but at least this gets the implementation moving forward. This is why every project needs an IC.

PARTNERING

Partnering is the concept of actively seeking someone else to accept responsibility for the tasks that some group has tossed over the wall. Normally when groups do this, these tasks get treated like diseased orphans. It's one of the IC's jobs to educate the group to the fact that it has a responsibility to find another group to *partner up* and take over these tasks.

The tale goes on: The IC challenged WUYS's stance by asking, "With whom did you *partner up* in the organization to take over the tasks you've rejected? In particular, who's going to build this history file?" WUYS was stunned by this concept. The IC had brought to the group's attention that there was a major problem here. The group's personnel needed to think in terms of what it meant to the rest of the corporation when they built the wall around their system, thereby limiting the scope of their work in ways that could be damaging to the organization.

The WUYS group accepted the IC's challenge, and with the IC's help started looking around and asking, "Where does this task belong in the organization?" WUYS got into the business of maintaining history because of historical precedences; it had evolved out of another system that used to maintain the history. Logically, the history belonged to the systems that owned the transactions, and so the WUYS group and the IC figured out that this transactions group, WMH (We Made History), should own the task. However, WMH had the reputation of being a bottleneck within the organization when it came to implementing any new products. If the tasks were left to them, nothing would get implemented.

The IC then called an all-systems-wide Architectural Review to determine who was going to build and maintain the history. The IC and Project Manager made a presentation at the Architectural Review about why this file was needed. As usual, there were nit-picking technical types who needed to be taken back to "square one" with a description of the current architectures, the historical precedences, and the nature of the current problem. And the IC and Project Manager needed to answer all those questions like, "Why can't you just do this?"—questions that had already been asked and answered umpteen times before. As a result, the Architectural Review did NOT resolve the issue, and the participants advised the IC to do some more research.

REDUCING DEPENDENCY

When an IC is confronted with a situation in which no amount of negotiation or mediation is going to get a person or group to accept responsibility for a task, she starts looking around for someone else to take over that task. By finding someone else (or assigning it to herself) to accept responsibility for the task, the IC can *reduce dependency* on that person or group who has been holding her hostage by not doing their part. *Reducing dependency* is one of the most powerful techniques in the IC's tool kit. ICs don't beat themselves up trying to convince some intransigent person or group to do something that they probably should do but in fact never will. ICs *reduce their dependency* by removing the obstinate party from the implementation loop. Nothing is more liberating than getting that person or group out of your hair. You will leap for joy!

The tale goes on: The IC was at an impasse. More research was never going to solve the problem of who should build and maintain the WUYS history file. To get the ball rolling, the IC needed to *reduce dependency* on WUYS, and work out a deal with some other group to step forward and accept responsibility for building and maintaining the history file. You can make a business case for just about any group owning a given task. So the IC went politicking! She soon sold the people in the WWDI (We Will Do It) group on the prospect of becoming heroes throughout the corporation by building the history file. And it turned out that WWDI could do it with considerably less effort than the WUYS group said it could. So the WWDI group would look great, not only for building the history but for doing it for less than the WUYS budget amount. And that's what happened. The WUYS group (and the WMH group) were bypassed in the implementation process; the WWDI group built the file, and its management garnered a lot of acclaim and prestige useful for political advantage. And the IC got her implementation done in a timely manner, owing to the strategy of *reducing dependency*.

POLICY AND PROCEDURES

The different policies and procedures of each group can have a dramatic impact on any implementation. In the preceding tale, the management of WUYS had grown the group into a monolithic bureaucracy strapped with convoluted policies and procedures. The WUYS estimate for building the history file, based on their modus operandi, was three years. The WWDI group, which the IC instigated, did the job in seven months even though it was also doing a major rearchitectural design of its own system at the time. This IC took the time to learn each group's policies and procedures. Then she determined how these might impact her implementation. When it became necessary, she figured out where to go to reduce dependency on the group that was hanging up her implementation.

ORPHANED TASKS

Finding homes for *orphaned tasks* is essential to the implementation process. These orphaned tasks invariably surface, and can be identified, during an implementation. Everyone knows these tasks are important and that they must get done. What's at issue is who is going to do them. ICs have guidelines for determining where tasks should be domiciled.

Finding Homes for Orphaned Tasks:
1. Who has to expend the least amount of energy to fulfill the task?
2. Who is the logical person or group to do this task?
3. Who will own the results of this task?

THE BUSINESS USER AND INFORMATION SYSTEMS

The business user as Project Manager in the modern organization must become knowledgeable about information systems in order to make intelligent and informed decisions. It's politically expedient for the IC to spur and maybe even prod the business user to become informed.

For example, a typical programming problem in the distributed processing environment would have the programmer asking the business user questions like, "For this transaction I must update four databases. I've updated three but I can't get to the fourth because the line is down. What do you (the business user) want me to do? Back-out the other three updates? Hold the fourth update until that database becomes available? What should I tell the workstation operator?—that I can't process the transaction or that I processed some of the transaction?" Providing the answers is not the programmer's decision; it's the *business user's call.*

Therefore, business users must move further into the technical world of information systems to comprehend these types of situations and understand what their options are, if they are to make decisions intelligently. The IC can be tremendously useful in this process by facilitating between the business user and the technical issues at hand.

OWNING ISSUES

When the business user also takes the role of Project Manager, it's best to entrust the IC with the implementation and direct the IC to keep the business user informed. However, problems will arise if the business user tries to micro-manage the implementation. The business user who wants to deal with every implementation issue should rightfully *own those issues*. Every issue should have only one owner. So either the IC owns it or the Project Manager owns it, but not both. Competent ICs just want to coordinate the implementation and they can't do that if they don't own the issues. This isn't a question of ego but rather a question of responsibility. If an issue has two owners, the danger is that one will make commitments that the other must uphold. This is political dynamite. The optimum situation is when the business user as Project Manager checks the pulse of the implementation but at the same time lets the IC own and resolve all the issues.

POLITICS OF VENDORS

It's in the very nature of selling that vendors will go to great lengths to ingratiate themselves to a client. Many times these clients become enamored and even dependent on the vendor. Once a person or group is hooked on a vendor, it's really difficult to get them motivated to "shop around." However, there are instances in which the IC must get the Project Manager and/or business user to test the market for products, features, and prices. Obviously the IC must spend the time and effort to stay abreast of the information technology market so she doesn't send someone looking for products and features that don't exist.

POLITICS OF TOOLS

Implementation "tools" are computer software products that support any aspect of the System Development Life Cycle. ICs have found one thing to be true about tools: If people want a certain tool, it will be in use everywhere; and if people don't, it won't be used anywhere. If someone within the organization has to fight for senior-level sponsorship of a tool, conduct seminars to sell the tool's alleged benefits, and then encourage any and everyone to use it, it's probably not a good product. The really useful tools are the ones that the organization couldn't stamp out if it wanted to. People will obtain the tools they really want, even buying them with their own money, if necessary. Programmers have even cannibalized existing tools to gain some additional functionality they desire. ICs stay in touch with the people doing the work so they can support the tools that are in favor with the implementation participants.

THE POLITICS OF "CASE"

Computer Aided Software Engineering (CASE) is not going to do away with or solve all the problems of system development and implementation. With a booming economy, you would probably see ever-bigger information systems budgets. In that case, there would also be time and resources to refine the systems development process. However, in the present struggling economy, competition amongst businesses is creating a cutthroat situation, with a narrowing and thinning of the field. If anything, information systems budgets are being slashed even as senior management expects ICs to hasten the time to implementation. Given this environment, sophisticated and expensive CASE tools with large learning curves aren't relevant. They just aren't solving business problems.

While CASE is brilliant in concept, it has been ravaged by its *implementation*. Vendors took a technology that could have been marketed and used like a word processor or spreadsheet, and then packed, priced, and sold it as the panacea for all the problems of the information systems industry. The marketing types obviously think that if a technological tool can solve all your problems, it must be expensive and have a lot of rules. It's too bad that a good technol-

Computers are like the God of the Old Testament. Lots of rules and no mercy.

—Joseph Campbell

ogy that was really needed never got going because of voracious marketing and hype.

OVER/UNDER FORMALIZE

ICs have found problems with implementations in which the systems professionals want to over-formalize the process with super-sophisticated CASE tools. In JIP Sessions you'll hear them say things like, "We must put all this into our CASE tool." There's nothing wrong with that, except it's a process that can take forever. Sometimes the IC will respond, "Why? Can't we just design a record layout and share it among ourselves?" The most important issue is to understand the business and get everything agreed upon in the Implementation Workbook, not spend everyone's time in the service of the CASE tool.

ICs have also found problems with implementations in which the systems gurus don't want to formalize anything. If an implementation is under-formalized then misunderstandings and miscommunications will abound. The opportunities for mismatched expectations are rampant. So the IC has to walk a fine line between over- and under-formalizing the implementation process. Over-formalize the implementation, and you miss the due date by months. Under-formalize the implementation, and what you implement (if anything) probably isn't what the business user needs.

DYSFUNCTIONAL ORGANIZATION

Can an IC be effective in a dysfunctional organization? What typifies a dysfunctional organization is the lack of structure. ICs have been effective in dysfunctional organizations, but only after putting some structure in place. One of the never-ending (and ever-tiring) tasks of the IC is being the person who holds on tight to the structure of the implementation. When somebody says, "Golly, do we really need to meet that date?" the IC is the person who says "Yes—even if we have to drive a stake in the ground and chain the malingerers to it."

IC'S RELATIONSHIP WITH ORGANIZATIONAL PERSONNEL

It is common for some people to feel that the IC is overstepping bounds, particularly if things aren't going well.

Once upon an implementation, things were going badly, so one manager called the IC and screamed, "You shouldn't have called that JIP Session. You're out of line." In this situation the IC just rolled with the verbal punch, knowing the manager was wrong. Calling the JIP Session was exactly what was needed, despite raising some bruises on managerial protocol. Interestingly, none of the management up the chain of command disagreed with what the IC was doing.

Once upon an implementation, the job involved rolling out a product to many sites over a period of months. The process was going too slowly, and the IC figured out that the problem resided in the initial generation of each workstation's database. In this co-operative processing environment, the database contained the terminal ID, the user ID, and the systems on the mainframe to which connection was required. Once the database was initialized with the pertinent information, a couple of programs were executed to configure the workstation. Since the implementation was going so slowly and the people who were supposed to be doing the generations were unable to do the work at that time, the IC volunteered to do the generations—which it had been predicted would take one month for each workstation.

With no instruction or support, the IC read the installation manual and started doing the generations. One Friday evening, she collided with a user training session on the wide area network (WAN). Because the IC and the training session were contending for resources, the system response time was seriously degraded. The IC didn't know that the trainers had gone to a lot of trouble to set up their training session statewide. The trainers figured out where the IC was by polling the network, and then called to ask her to get off the system. However, not knowing she was impacting a number of people statewide, the IC told the trainers to wait while she finished the generations. The person in charge of the trainers got on the phone and started screaming obscenities at the IC. It was nasty.

The upshot of the whole affair was that the IC proved the generations could be done in one week. Ironically, the person who bellowed at the IC was the same person who was telling senior management that each generation would take a month. So the IC was going to be at odds with that person sooner or later anyway.

Management was delighted that the IC proved the generations could be done so quickly; the other person ended up changing jobs and ultimately left the organization. The moral of the story: If you're doing what needs to be done to get the product implemented, more often than not everything will work out for the best.

PICK YOUR IMPLEMENTATIONS

If you would be an effective IC, you must learn to turn down work. Specifically, don't get caught in a project with a system or product that is impossible to implement. The key to a successful career as an IC is to choose your implementations wisely. Pick one that needs to be done with a style of your own. Then go for it and watch yourself become a star.

Once upon an implementation, the IC turned down a Project Manager who wanted her for a project on the "bleeding edge" of technology. In the IC's professional opinion the project was a long way from implementation even though vendors were responding to the client's Request For Proposal (RFP). Vendors will readily respond to a risky RFP because it's a chance for them to develop a product with the client's money. What the Project Manager should have been soliciting was Proof of Concept (POC) from the vendors. Let the vendors prove they have the technology to perform the task before they respond to a Request For Proposal. This doesn't mean the project couldn't use a coordinator. The organization just needed to understand that their project was a long way from implementation and, therefore, hiring a Research and Development Coordinator (R&DC) would probably be more appropriate than hiring an IC.

SURVIVAL

Staying with a dead-end implementation can be embarrassing and bad for your reputation. You must decide whether it's worth it, and also whether it's even feasible to get out. Sometimes you can't leave but you can keep a diary to record everything that happens. Then, at the Post-Implementation Review you will have a document detailing your perceptions and opinions of events as they occurred. Even when an implementation is going "straight down the tubes," you can still learn a lot. Accentuate the positive. That's the challenge.

If you're on a dead-end implementation you can always try spending some of your political capital to effect a change. However, you only have so much capital, so you must determine how much of it you're willing to gamble in an attempt to make changes. *It's all about choices.* If you go for it and fail, all you've done is alienated people.

WAITING

The most difficult response to a political situation (a conflict based on personalities, not merit) is *to do nothing*. Ironically, many times the most appropriate action is inaction. As emotional beings, we all react to being unjustly implicated or accused. However, acting on that impulse can exacerbate the situation and, more often than not, make it worse. So to be an effective IC and survive politically, you must learn to *wait*. "Playing the waiting game" may seem useless but it's really the art of remaining inactive in anticipation of better circumstances. If you have the patience and persistence to wait out a politically sticky situation, an opportunity will occur to vindicate or remove yourself.

> *Waiting is not merely empty hoping. It is the inner certainty of knowing you can reach your goal.*
>
> —The Book of Changes

CHAPTER 11

Quality: How to Assure It in the Implementation

Information systems organizations are having their budgets pared, their project schedules squeezed, and their expectations of quality increased. ICs must now deliver systems or products with higher quality, in less time and with fewer resources.

> Now that most backshopping processes have been automated in the information systems industry, the two big issues will be the user interface and quality.
>
> —Jack Hancock

It's important to understand how information systems are different from other industries. Unlike manufacturing with its repetitive processes, every system or product implementation is unique. If every implementation had some commonality, each successive effort would be better than the one before. However, every implementation deals with changing business processes and transitioning the business user to the new system or product. So it's impossible to do the same implementation twice—even in the same organization.

INSTITUTING QUALITY IN THE IMPLEMENTATION PROCESS

In the information systems industry, the standard practice for measuring quality is to appraise the software after development. Typically, defects or errors in the programming code are quantified and measured after it's implemented. However, software developers have no standard measures of utility, so statistical analysis is imprecise at best and often meaningless. To be effective, the procedures for assuring quality should *precede* the implementation. Once a system or product has been implemented, it's too late (at least for you as the IC) to do anything about it anyway. You need to institute quality into the *implementation process*.

> *The quality of the product is governed by the quality of the process.*
>
> —Watts Humphries

The quality thesis that has been used successfully by ICs was introduced by Dr. Walter Shewhart in 1925 at Bell Telephone Laboratories. It has since become known as "Continuous Process Improvement." The Japanese have also employed this concept with great success, and call it by a single word: *kaizen*.

> Kaizen *means gradual, unending improvement.*
>
> —Masaaki Imai

Continuous Process Improvement is a circular process that is iterative, much like the Software Development Model. It involves recognizing and identifying a problem. (It doesn't have to be a problem; it could just be an inherent weakness or inefficiency.) After identification comes brainstorming, deciding upon, and implementing a solution. Finally, the results are verified to determine whether the solution produces the desired effect. If not, then you reiterate the entire process. Figure 11.1 is the Continuous Improvement Process model with its six phases: recognize, identify, brainstorm, devise, implement, and verify.

The key to this perspective on quality is to continually seek to find and *improve the process* of implementation. ICs are always asking, reminding, and supporting anyone who has ideas about how to improve the implementation process—because the process itself determines the quality of the system or product to be implemented. ICs know that their encouragement brings good results; it's something they've witnessed many times. Implementation participants

Figure 11.1.   Continuous Improvement Process Model

are always assessing the implementation process and coming up with suggestions that positively impact the level of quality.

Software Development Model

Philip Crosby says that quality is *"conformance to requirements."* The key to this perspective on quality is that the job be done right the first time. Rework is excessively expensive and unnecessary if this precept of quality is adhered to from a project's inception. This definition of quality is great for the building and construction industries. Get it right the first time, and no costly do-overs! However, the development of information systems has become an iterative process that bears little resemblance to the so-called "waterfall" model that use to prevail in the information systems industry and is still prevalent in the construction industries. In the waterfall model, once a project phase is done, it's difficult and expensive to go back—like water falling off the edge. But how do you "do it right the first time" when you're prototyping? The Software Development Model of today is circular and iterative. Figure 11.2 is the Soft-

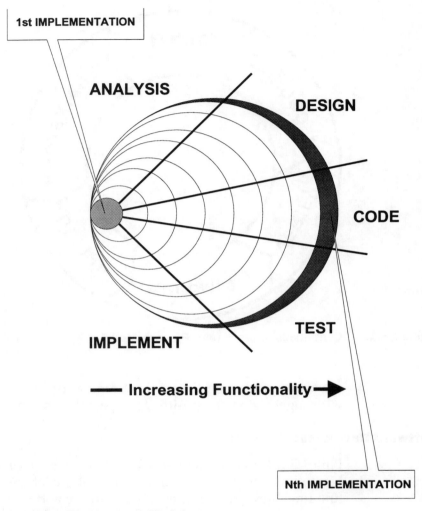

Figure 11.2.   Software Development Model

ware Development Model and illustrates the iterative nature of developing and implementing a system.

> *Software development is an iterative process.*
>
> —*Roger Pressman*

Customer Satisfaction

Customer satisfaction (as a measure of quality) is an issue every implementation must address. Joseph Jaran says quality is *"fitness for purpose."* The key to this perspective on customer satisfaction is that the product will do what it's expected to do, regardless of how it's done. So the customer may not understand what's going on, but she expects the product to perform with the functionality she desires. W. Edwards Demming says quality is *"meeting or exceeding customer expectations,"* even if the customer isn't aware of what those expectations are. The suppositions about customers' expectations are the key to this perspective on customer satisfaction. While both Jaran's and Demming's points of view on quality are sound, their differences are without distinction. The point of both theses is *customer satisfaction*.

In some industries, quality as a responsibility is espoused at every level of the organization. For example, auto assembly plants place signs on the factory floor that state, "Customer Satisfaction Begins Here." Can you imagine a computer programmer believing that customer satisfaction begins with his or her code? Programmers typically have some consciousness of the business user, but never the customer. Too often programmers and other technical specialists believe customer satisfaction is the responsibility of the organizational personnel who actually interact with the customers. Therefore, the burden falls on the IC to promote customer satisfaction as a concept and show how quality can be an action item by recognizing those who do improve on the implementation process.

Worker Involvement

In the automotive industry, the factories are retooled every two or three years. This is why quality (continuous process improvement) is so important. Once the new hardware is installed, the people working the line are the ones who make improvements in the assembly process. The engineers who designed the new hardware used the latest modeling techniques and incorporated ergonomic factors into their design, but they couldn't possibly envision everything. The burden of process improvement therefore is borne by the workers on the line, who can recognize problems and offer suggestions to improve and expedite the assembly process. These improvements translate into tremendous savings in terms of worker productivity, time lost to injury, and the elimination of defects. Some assembly plants mandate that each employee must make a specified number of suggestions per year. Their managers are required to spend several hours each week reading those suggestions. Most of the suggestions are usually implemented. ICs try to bring this same determination to their implementations. They're always querying everyone about potential problems with the implementation, and seeking ways in which the implementation effort could be improved.

Process Maturity

The Software Engineering Institute (SEI) has developed what it calls the Process Maturity Model. If you examine it, you will see five levels of "process maturity" pertaining to information systems project management. ICs find most organizations they work for are somewhere between levels one and two, and wistfully longing for level three. Figure 11.3 is a variant of the Software Engineering Institute's Process Maturity Model with its five stages: chaotic, intuitive, defined, managed, and optimized.

The Software Engineering Institute's own research shows that over 70 percent of all organizations are at level one, which represents an immature process. If an organization's process maturity is somewhere between chaotic and intuitive, it's reasonable to assume that the quality of the systems and products being developed (and the implementation process itself) is probably not good. Therefore, ICs are continually trying to instill quality as a concept; theirs is a grass-roots effort to proselytize everyone they work with on an implementation.

Commitment vs. Compliance

One of the frustrations ICs commonly deal with is the mind-set that every utterance of senior management has more value than anything the personnel down the chain of command might say. ICs promote the view that it's important and appropriate for thinking people to evaluate what they hear, using criteria based on their *own* experience and knowledge. For an implementation to be effective, the IC needs participants who can decide upon, for themselves, the most appropriate course of action. However, many times during implementations, ICs hear questions like, "What did the senior manager say? What does the boss want? How can we make the manager happy?" When people are in this mode, they aren't cre-

Figure 11.3. **SEI's Process Maturity Model**

atively engaged in the implementation process, they aren't employing their expertise, and they aren't thinking for themselves. It's the difference between commitment and compliance. For an effective implementation, ICs need committed people. If they're merely compliant, they won't be creative and they won't "go the extra mile." If you forget to tell them to do something, they won't take the initiative and see that it gets done anyway.

One of the IC's responsibilities is to get every participant involved with the implementation, and you can do this by democratizing the implementation process—by letting everyone know they can all make contributions to the implementation process. As professionals working for the organization, the implementation participants possess the business and information systems knowledge-base to make improvements on a par with anyone. Therefore, the IC elicits their energy and enthusiasm, and facilitates the outpouring of their ideas and solutions to improve on the quality of the implementation.

Quality as an Agenda Item

At JIP Status Sessions (described in Chapter 8), it's a good practice for ICs to discuss *quality* as an agenda item. You can ask, "How can we *improve* what we are currently doing?" or "What can we do tomorrow to surpass what we did today?" For example, you might say, "Folks, the Issue Log is too damned short! Let's come up with more issues that we can deal with right now." And sure enough, someone will come up with real *issues*—which now identified, can be dealt with before they become problems.

The road to quality is paved with bricks personally placed by everyone who works on the project; this is continuous improvement. Technical specialists and IC professionals are modern knowledge-workers who are cooperatively committed to incorporating quality into whatever they do. This means being personally motivated to continuously improve yourself and your job performance for the betterment of your organization and your society. Trying to improve every day also makes for a more exciting implementation effort, and this kind of excitement can be contagious.

Implementing Quality vs. Assigning Blame

When an implementation is bungled, instead of having a Post-Implementation Review that attempts to ascertain who did what wrong and then assigning blame, try searching for ways to improve on the quality of the implementation process. Mistakes that are made in any organization's intricate implementation process often result from misunderstandings about that process. The problem is not a matter of negligence or incompetence on the part of the implementation participants; it is more a matter of the quality of the implementation procedures. So to assure that future implementations are more fail-safe, work on the quality issues instead of seeking culprits.

Management of User Expectations

One thing that really differentiates information systems from other industrial disciplines is that the expectations of what an information system can deliver are limitless. In most businesses, if you ask for something outrageous, you will be told that it can't be done—and there will be proven business cases to substantiate that opinion. However, this is rarely the case in information systems. No matter how fantastic the request, the potential buyers expect their requests to be taken seriously and, in most cases, delivered. Information systems personnel are reluctant to deny any request because information technology is still immature and in a state of tremendously rapid evolution. There is little precedence and virtually no benchmarks to substantiate that any user request is necessarily ridiculous.

> *Software is malleable and changeable. Therefore it absorbs functionality.*
>
> *—Stan Rifkin*

Even so, the IC need not accede to every demand. As the IC, part of your responsibility to the quality of the implementation process is to *manage user expectations*. You also see to it that the Change Management Team isn't hounded from pillar to post, or buried in an avalanche of Change Requests. If you fail to manage expectations and effectively quash the superfluous Change Requests, the operational effectiveness of the Change Management Team will be destroyed and the quality of the implementation seriously degraded.

Do Overs

It's disturbing for ICs to witness the many implementations in which the organization doesn't have time or funding for the procedures associated with quality—such as adequate design of the system to be developed, proper training for the business users, thorough testing, and much more. However, these same organizations always seem to find the time and money for "do overs." The infamous "do over" refers to the process of correcting the problem you created by not adhering to the principles of quality. ICs who are involved in "do overs" tend to become mired in endless nuisance work that is a direct result of their organization's haphazard procedures. You find that you're curing the symptoms, not the disease—and more importantly, you're not resolving the underlying business problems on which the success of the implementation depends.

CONCLUSION

An organization's culture is hard to change. Old work habits are deeply ingrained, so trying to bring quality to the implementation process can be a daunting task. There may even be some persons participating in the implementation effort who are willing to sacrifice the quality of the implementation for the sake of their own agenda. Dedicated ICs are interested in implementations done with quality in mind, even when that isn't politically expedient. Quality is a goal worthy of any IC's aspirations. Any mediocre knowledge worker can front a mediocre implementation of a mediocre system or product. However, it takes a professional to coordinate a quality implementation of a product or system that is truly responsive to the business user's needs.

CHAPTER 12

Implementation Coordination:
Its Practical Application

The information systems industry has reached the point where its practitioners can build systems larger than they can manage. Information systems professionals are becoming overwhelmed with their own system's complexity. These systems generate more information than these professionals and their business users can assimilate, promote change faster than they can conform to it, and create greater interdependency than they can effectively administer.

Incompatibility looms everywhere in today's intricate heterogeneous systems-environments. Languages, architectures, and communication protocols are all mismatched to some extent. If you're attempting an implementation that encompasses dissimilar technologies controlled by different groups within the organization, you've got trouble. Your only hope for success is via explicit coordination and facilitated negotiation amongst the various groups. JIP Sessions are the forum for effectively coordinating groups and personnel, and the IC is the facilitator who negotiates which system paradigm will be implemented.

NEW DEVELOPMENT

What ICs have noticed in large organizations is that there isn't much new development. Typically, large organizations have very mature product lines that are supported by archaic legacy systems. Organizations with legacy systems would love to dump them and migrate to object-oriented databases executing on pen-based platforms networked through cellular modems. However, these legacy systems are the heart of the organization's information repository and, as such, cannot be risked on the "bleeding edge" of technology. So what we have are organizations mixing and matching new technologies with the old, like the classic case of putting a Graphical User Interface (GUI) on an existing mainframe system.

While some people would call building a Graphical User Interface "new development," ICs observe that programmers are building GUIs that conform to and replace the screen layouts of a resident legacy system. Then the business user(s) can create, update, or delete a transaction with the new GUI, which still communicates with the same old legacy system on the mainframe. What you've really got is a new front-end combined with the tweaking of resident legacy systems on the back-end. The tricky part isn't the programming but rather the coordination of all the interfaces among the new front-ends and the back-end legacy systems. Integrating into the existing legacy systems is difficult because these resident applications typically aren't well-documented. This is how the JIP Sessions can be profoundly beneficial. By getting all the principals in one room, you can build on everyone's application knowledge and devise workable implementation strategies.

If they could, most software engineers would prefer to work on a "blank sheet of paper." This means working on an information system from its inception. Most of the literature on systems development and project management in the industry also approach information systems from this perspective of every system beginning anew. The comparison would be housing construction in which every unit is built from the ground up. Each house is an independent entity.

However, information systems are typically interdependent. If you extrapolate the concept of interdependence to housing construction, it would be like having every house *ever* built as a part of every house *being* built. Inheritance and mutual dependence are commonplace. In the real world of interdependent legacy systems, it's a rare IC's luxury to be able to start from the "mythical" beginning of the Systems Development Life Cycle. Instead, what you find is an information maze that involves new programming, modification programming, and down and dirty "kluging"—whatever it takes to get a new system or product implemented. JIP Sessions provide the perfect forum for handling disparate information systems and dissimilar technologies: they bring the implementation participants together (with the IC's facilitation) so that they can start generating solutions to amazingly thorny problems. With over 90 billion lines of COBOL code in use today, there has to be a tremendous amount of modification and "kluging" of these legacy systems to fulfill all the requirements and requests of the business users.

COOPERATIVE PROCESSING

Cooperative processing is a distributed information system architecture that has a programmable machine (such as a personal computer or workstation) on the front-end and typically a mainframe or mini-computer on the back-end. In distributed and hardware heterogeneous environments, the layers of the organization will tend to argue with one another about which job belongs to whom—such as who sets the standard, who can change the standard, and who maintains the standard.

> *Animosity between personal computer personnel and mainframe personnel is a fact of life in any large organization today. Getting these two groups to cooperate is a diplomatic coup because each side wants to dominate.*
>
> —*John Tibbetts and Barbara Bernstein,*
> Building Cooperative Processing Applications Using SAA

Since culture-clashes between PC and mainframe personnel are inevitable in the implementation of a cooperative processing architecture, cooperation between the various groups is paramount. ICs have a good success rate in coordinating these implementations; they resolve differences among the various groups, getting them to move forward in a systematic and disciplined manner. Without an IC to effectively orchestrate everyone's effort, animosity and distrust can run rife among the various organizational groups and ultimately overwhelm an implementation.

Once upon an implementation, the IC worked for an organization that used a business-critical information system named WAM (What A Mess), which comprised numerous mainframe applications. The WAM system was used every day and had been developed over the years on a combination of several different vendors' hardware platforms. To take an order, the order-entry personnel who used the WAM system had to go from one mainframe application to another. The WAM system had evolved into a three-headed monster that required every order-entry clerk to use several terminals just to log onto the multifarious applications. Then the organization developed networking and teleprocessing software that enabled the order-entry clerks to work on a single terminal and just "hot-key" from one application to another. But the clerks still had to log-off and then log-on as they hot-keyed from application to application. All this was time-consuming. Statistical analysis showed it took an order-entry clerk an average of 30 minutes to handle a single order. It was evident that any improvement in this customer-contact time would improve profitability enormously.

The organization decided to install personal computers with an object-oriented GUI on the front-end of every application. The old WAM system was made up of archaic online systems that were driven with character-based codes (such as 45978, 34587, and so forth), which the order-entry clerks had been entering on dumb terminals. The Implementation Plan called for the installation a new WAM system with an object-oriented GUI for the business-user interface that used icons, scroll bars, and radio knobs instead of cryptic character codes.

If the implementation was successful, this new business-user interface (object-oriented GUI) would lead the order-entry clerks through the ordering process and enable them to easily navigate the WAM system. The order-entry clerks' customer-contact time would be substantially shortened. And the use of object-oriented technology would also reduce the time required to train new order-entry clerks. The organization would also be more profitable because the increased efficiency of the order-entry clerks would free them for the business of selling products (instead of slowly stumbling around the old WAM system). Finally, the new business-user interface would also decrease errors by reducing the complexity of handling a order.

In addition to the object-oriented GUI, the Implementation Plan called for each personal computer to have application-initialization software that was configured to automatically log-on to every mainframe application that the order-entry clerk normally accessed. This would eliminate the time-consuming process of logging-on and -off these applications one at a time. This application-initialization software would automatically execute when the personal computer was booted each morning, and the clerk would be simultaneously logged-on to multiple applications.

The IC was assigned to this project only after the implementation effort had been bumbling along for several months. The IC's charter was to implement the new front-end, organization-wide, into the cooperative processing architecture. This consisted of implementing the object-oriented GUI, configuring the application-initialization software for each order-entry clerk, and installing software on each personal computer that reformatted each transaction to resemble what the old back-end WAM system had previously received.

One of the implementation's constraints was to restrict changes in the mainframe application programs or databases, insofar as possible. Senior management insisted that each sales order be formatted on the personal computer to look just like a transaction coming from the old dumb terminals. So the object-oriented GUI front-end only captured the order and then software was used to reformat that order into a transaction that was shipped to the old WAM system on the back-end.

Before the IC was assigned to this project, each order-entry clerk was responsible for configuring the application-initialization software to his or her personal computer. And each order-entry clerk's application-initialization software was uniquely configured because every clerk had different sales and ordering responsibilities. Due to these differences, each clerk signed-on to a different configuration of applications within the WAM system. To configure the application-initialization software, there were a number of different systems groups that each order-entry clerk had to work with, and a myriad of procedures that were not obvious, not easily explained, and not really understood by most of the clerks.

The process of implementing the object-oriented programming code, the configuration of the application-initialization software, and the installation of the transaction-reformatting software became known as the "PC Gen" (personal computer generation). Before a "PC Gen" could be done, the order-entry clerk's functions had to be identified so that the application-initialization software could be configured for that particular clerk's responsibilities.

To support the object-oriented GUI, some changes to the back-end WAM applications was necessary. The implementation of these changes proved to be logistically difficult because the changes impacted the way the business users conducted their business. This was exactly what senior management wanted to avoid. In large organizations, it's difficult to communicate the extent of the changes being made in a single night to its thousands of business users, and the risk in making such a change is enormous.

The IC really proved her worth and the value of JIP Sessions because she was able to successfully orchestrate this very complex cooperative processing architecture implementation with thousands of "PC Gens" that took over a year to complete. First, the IC used JIP Implementation Planning Sessions to negotiate a settlement between the personal-computer and mainframe personnel about which group was accountable for specific areas of responsibility (such as standards, record formatting, interchange codes, messaging traffic, and so forth). The IC had to tactfully ensure that no group felt dominated by any other. Second, the IC facilitated many other JIP Sessions before the "PC Gen" process was clearly defined and procedures established. Third, the IC called numerous JIP Interface Design Sessions to coordinate the horrendous logistical issues between the existing back-end WAM applications and the front-end personal computers being brought online with the new business-user interface (the object-oriented GUI). For the IC, the entire implementation was a tremendous enterprise requiring diligence and communication skills in order to make sure that all the groups and various technologies were coordinated and effectively implemented.

CLIENT/SERVER

Client/server is a hierarchical architecture that is constrained to the *client asking*, and the *server responding*. This request/reply protocol is usually implemented on a Local Area Network (LAN). When facilitating JIP Implementation Planning Sessions for client/server implementations, ICs must be careful that the participants don't get hung up on the technological aspects of putting the network together. Client/server implementations shouldn't be about technology; they should be about the business *behind* the technology. What needs to be implemented is an integrated business environment that takes into consideration the technical issues.

There is no "one size fits all" when it comes to implementing client/server environments, because each one is unique—not in terms of its technology, but rather in how it's *implemented*. The IC is responsible for ensuring that a business environment is implemented, not just for the installation of a Local Area Network. Depending on the business user's requirements, the IC's approach may differ. Obviously, there are some common aspects to every client/server implementation. For instance, there is only one way to wire the Local Area Network together. However, every client/server implementation is unique in terms of the business user's needs.

Once upon an implementation, an organization was down-sizing several applications that resided on a mainframe computer to a client/server environment running on a Local Area Network. The mainframe's resident applications weren't providing the flexibility that the business user required. In the mainframe environment it wasn't easy for the business users to copy, cut, and paste data into their reports, spreadsheets, and other documents. Tools to support this kind of functionality weren't available on the mainframe but were available in the client/server environment.

The first action of the Project Manager (from the business side of the organization) was to have a Local Area Network installed. The Project Manager's implementation strategy (such as it was) then called for everyone to install whatever word processor, spreadsheet, or other software package they wanted on their personal computers. Before very long, this strategy began creating replicating inefficiencies. For example, the client/server environment soon had five different versions of the same vendor's word processor on the network.

This was when senior management assigned an IC to coordinate the implementation for the Project Manager. The IC suggested to the Project Manager, "Instead of just installing a Local Area Network, why don't we try JIP Sessions as a forum for reengineering your business, using everyone's input? Then we can devise a comprehensive Implementation Plan." The IC facilitated the JIP Implementation Planning Sessions, in which the Project Manager and other participants soon devised a different implementation strategy. The new plan called for all software to be domiciled on the file server. Everyone on the network would then be accessing the same version or level of the application software (word processors, spreadsheets, communications, or whatever). The ability to access all applications from the file server made this very different from the original implementation strategy.

Using the JIP Sessions, the business user was able to identify new opportunities for doing business differently. Data that previously wasn't being captured on the mainframe would now be collected as part of the business user's daily operations on the personal computer. The business user also identified some new business practices that could be used to gain a competitive advantage. It formerly took the business users weeks to get certain specified data off the mainframe. With the client/server environment, this same data was online and available at all times. The business user would have an integrated process that allowed the data to be easily assessed for generating electronic reports, developing spreadsheets, and/or performing interactive analysis. Then this same data, with its associated reports and spreadsheets, could be compressed and electronically shipped to the home office. The home office could then load the data directly into their information system. Before the implementation of the client/server environment, the business user had to print all the reports and mail them to the home office, where the data then had to be rekeyed for input into the home office's computer.

BUSINESS-PROCESS REENGINEERING

The challenge in the information systems industry over the next decade is to *reduce processing time*. Reengineering the business procedures and implementing those changes in the application code are the keys to mitigating the substantial time constraints now associated with information systems processing.

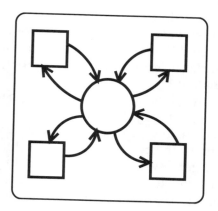

Business-process reengineering analyzes the business from the enterprise level. Most analysis in information systems occurs at the application level. The problem with application systems analysis is that it's detail-oriented. You can't see the complex systemic problems affecting an entire company if you look at information systems at just the application level. For reengineering the complex problems of information systems, the view is much better at the enterprise level, that is, looking at the business as an organic whole rather than as a collection of parts.

Business-process reengineering does not deal with hardware or software per se. It's an issue of analyzing the organization's current business processes to determine what can be streamlined or even eliminated. It is also an issue of rethinking how the organization wants its *business to operate*. When reengineering its business, the organization eliminates some processes and comes up with new ones that work better or faster. This makes the organization more responsive to the customer and provides a mechanism for increasing sales.

> *Don't automate, obliterate.*
>
> —Michael Hammer

Invariably, when businesses automate they merely use the prevailing technologies to replicate what they are currently doing. The problem with this approach is that it simply automates all the business's existing inefficiencies and irrelevant processes. Historically, many processes in place in the business environment once had a reason for being and served their purpose well, but time and technology have rendered them inefficient or irrelevant. However, lacking any analysis, these processes tend to be perpetuated, not eliminated, by automation.

It would appear that business process reengineering should happen at the beginning of the Systems Development Life Cycle. So why are ICs involved in this process, since they are usually involved in the back-end of the cycle? The reason is that when some organizations actually get down to addressing the implementation issues, they realize that they haven't envisaged how the new system or product will integrate into their resident information systems and technologies. Therefore, the IC has to facilitate JIP Business Process ReEngineering Sessions to model the organization's current work-flow. This gives the implementation a "road map" as well as a baseline from which to initiate implementation planning. Once an organization's work-flow has been modeled, the process of reengineering the business can be undertaken.

Once upon an implementation, the IC facilitated several JIP Business Process ReEngineering Sessions to help the organization model its business work-flow. The model that was developed contained several hundred business processes. Together, the IC and a team of knowledgeable persons in the organization then systematically attacked the credibility of each process. They found that many of the processes supported historical procedures that no longer existed. Although these procedures had been institutionalized into organizational policy, they were no longer relevant because the nature of the business had changed, or they were mandated by legal requirements that were no longer in force and, in some cases, they even supported outdated technologies such as pneumatic tubes and carbon copies. The IC and the JIP Session participants were able to reduce the number of business processes in the model by 75 percent! ICs find that these kinds of inefficiencies, which are supported by historical policies, tend to be the rule rather than the exception.

There is nothing new under the sun.

—King Solomon

A note about the modeling tools of business process reengineering: Ed Yourdon and Tom DeMarco's data flow diagrams (DFDs) are not a unique creation. They co-opted the DFD concept from "business engineering." The business engineering discipline called it *process flows* instead of *data flows*. Today you find that the reengineering gurus (such as Michael Hammer, and others) are using these same modeling techniques, which they call *business diagrams*. Figure 12.1 is an example of a Business Process Diagram. Information system personnel will recognize that the business process reengineering modeling and work-flow techniques are a variation on data flow diagrams.

Once upon an implementation, the IC facilitated JIP Business-Process ReEngineering Sessions for a bank that was concerned about its information systems data becoming so fragmented that its customer service was being impacted. By modeling the work-flow, the JIP Sessions participants were able to track a typical customer coming to the bank for several services. First, the customer wanted to open a checking account, so she had to see the account manager for that product. Second, she wanted to inquire about an auto loan, so she had to go to another office in the bank to see the loan officer for that product. Finally, she wanted to purchase some travelers checks, and had to go to yet another office in the building and deal with the special services representative. The JIP Session participants began to characterize this as the "fragmented customer" scenario.

The JIP Session discovered that the bank's data had become so voluminous and fragmented that it was becoming hard for the organization's information systems to manage that data at the customer level. The bank had gobs of account numbers representing different products that could all belong to one customer. The challenge for the JIP Session participants was to relate this fragmented data across the entire organization so that, as far as the customer was concerned, every account and transaction she had with the bank was seamlessly integrated.

By reengineering the business processes, the JIP Session participants were able to capitalize on new-found efficiencies to devise a data integration scheme. Afterwards, the "integrated customer" needed to talk with only one employee at the bank, who took care of all the customer's needs. The value to the customer is obvious, but the value to the bank was that its employees could now enhance the customer contact—by querying them about their needs and suggesting other services offered by the bank. This had a dramatic impact on the sale of products and services to the consumers.

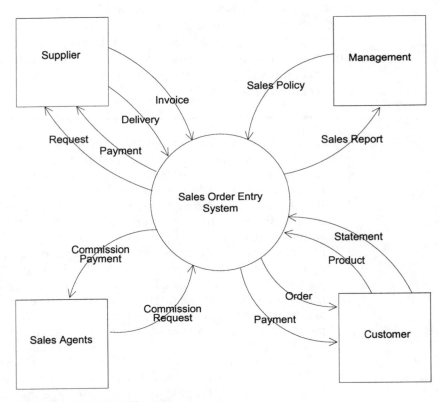

Figure 12.1.   Business Process Diagram

It's important when calling a JIP Business Process ReEngineering Session to make sure that information systems people are part of the JIP Session. One IC facilitated a JIP Business Process ReEngineering Session with only the people from the business side of the organization, with the result that the JIP Session produced a resolution saying, "We want the new system built with object technologies." Given the application's requirements, this was not only inappropriate, it was not even technologically feasible.

MERGING SYSTEMS AND DATA CENTERS

The need for an IC is never more evident than when there is a merger of information systems and/or data centers. Usually this happens when one organization buys or merges with another. The logistical problems in these types of implementations are enormous. ICs have facilitated JIP Sessions with over fifty people in attendance that conference called another JIP Session fifteen hundred miles away with over fifty people in that session! Facilitating multiple JIP Sessions concurrently over a conference phone call will really exercise your skills of orchestration. Mergers of systems and/or data centers are especially tough for the IC because there are so many unknowns. Typically, when an IC implements a system or product in the operational environment for an organization, that environment is stable and has other systems and products already in residence. So you know what you've got and where you're going. This is rarely the case with systems and/or data center mergers. Everything is unique to one or often to both the organizations. Moreover, a merger can dictate changes in an organization's systems that normally wouldn't be necessitated, such as upgrading all the software and/or hardware to support the systems and products being merged in.

ICs are indispensable for mergers if for no other reason than that they develop a standardized vocabulary between the personnel on both sides who are responsible for the systems and/or centers being merged. Like the Lilliputians and Blefuscuians, the antagonists in *Gulliver's Travels*, people are ready to go to war about something as trivial as which end should be cracked when an egg is broken. Organizational personnel can be just as petty about their organizational idioms and linguistic preferences. While this may seem trifling, it's not to be minimized. For purposes of a merger, ICs have had to spend weeks documenting terms and the definitions assigned to them. By ensuring that the personnel of both organizations utilize a common nomenclature, the IC knows that all the participants in the merger can communicate without ambiguity. Clear communication is a prerequisite for the success of any merger.

PACKAGED SOFTWARE

Due to application backlogs, limited staff, and the problems inherent in any systems development effort, many organizations opt to purchase packaged software from an outside vendor rather than develop a custom application themselves. After the requirements analysis and vendor selection process are complete, the purchased package must be implemented in the production environment. While the design, development, and application testing has been done by the outside vendor, the implementation of the package and the integration testing involving the organization's other systems pose just as many problems as any other implementation.

Typically, there are other groups in the organization who will be impacted by the package to be implemented. Because the usual phases of the System Development Life Cycle have been bypassed, these other groups sometimes won't even know that the business user intends to install a new application. The IC and the JIP Sessions have proven invaluable in this case, because the IC coordinates these other groups and solicits their support of the implementation for the first time. This can be a devilish situation that taxes the IC's facilitation and persuasion skills.

> Once upon an implementation, the IC was coordinating the implementation of an accounts payable package that did not perform with the functionality promised by the vendor. The IC coordinated all the Joint Integration Testing, thoroughly documenting each problem so that the vendor would be held accountable and couldn't say, "Oh, you didn't use the application correctly" or "That's not a bug, it's a feature."

TRAINING

Sometimes the IC's job isn't about coordinating the implementation of software and/or hardware. It can also be about coordinating the development of the supporting documentation and getting people organized to use a new system. This is what JIP Training Strategy Sessions are about.

Once upon an implementation, the IC was assigned to a project in which a "virtual network" allowed each personal computer to be logged on to a requested mainframe host from anywhere in the eastern United States. Although the organization had constructed this huge networking facility, it neglected to provide the personal-computer operators with any documentation for the network management tools. The IC's charter was to coordinate and facilitate the JIP Training Strategy Sessions so that documentation for the operators could be developed. Then she had to organize all the training for the operators so that they were prepared to use the network management tools when the virtual network was brought online.

IMPLEMENTATION COORDINATORS AND ORGANIZATIONAL CHANGE

ICs are partners and initiators for change. Change is a big issue because organizations are evaluating their application portfolios to find innovative ways to sell new products to customers. With the migration towards cooperative processing, organizations are redefining their human systems as well as reengineering their information systems. So the traditional way that organizations used to do business is not the way they will be doing business in the future.

Organizations are in trouble if they have to rely on thirty-year-old legacy systems to compete with the marketing expansion of foreign companies and the breakdown of inter-lattice competition (such as regulated public utilities). With old legacy systems, every time even a small change is made, something else breaks because no one really understands the interrelationships among the numerous applications' program code.

ICs are among the "agents for change" who are leading the way out of this quandary. Their ability to facilitate JIP Sessions is getting organization personnel together to resolve issues. JIP Sessions help organizations exploit new technologies so they can become more responsive to competitive pressures. The challenge for ICs is not only to support these changes but to be a major human factor in the organization's effort to accomplish these changes. Figure 12.2 is a symbolic representation of the communication and coordination an IC must exercise to promote organizational change and achieve successful implementations.

Figure 12.2.   Coordination/Communication Wheel

Index